FROM COOL RUNNINGS
TO WORLD SUPERPOWER

FROM COOL RUNNINGS TO WORLD SUPERPOWER

THE RISE OF AMERICAN FENCING

IGOR CHIRASHNYA

Copyright © 2019 by Igor Chirashnya

Cover design: Alexey Reznik

Cover photo: Augusto Bizzi

All rights reserved.

Printed in the United States of America

First Printing, 2019

ISBN 9781099911668

Cover photo: USA Team members and coaches celebrate double victory of American foil fencer Lauren Scruggs at 2019 Cadet and Junior World Championship in Torun, Poland. 16 years old Scruggs became the first American foilist, men or women, to win both Cadet and Junior world titles at the same championship. Lauren trains in the New York's Fencers Club and coached by Sean McClaine

Academy of Fencing Masters

86 Railway Ave.,

Campbell, CA 95008

https://academyoffencingmasters.com/

In memory of my father

Table of Contents

Preface 1
Chapter 1: Explosive Beginnings in the New World 7
Chapter 2: Extreme underdogs 15
    American fencing sputters 20
    Hiccups in the making a mark 24
Chapter 3: Close but Not Quite 31
    The changing face of American fencing 31
    Fueled by European fencing masters 34
    The importance of almost 38
Chapter 4: Tide turns in the 2000s 41
    America flips the switch on the World Championship 41
    Challenging at the Olympics 49
    Coming into our own 54
    Recent History's Huge Successes 55
Chapter 5: Fall of the Soviet Union 59
    The Soviet Republic 60
    Not really amateurs 62
    Military aspect 65
Chapter 6: New talent in the USA 71
    Flood of fencing professionals 72

Eastern bloc philosophy 77
International nature of sport in USA 79
Chapter 7: Niche Nature 81
How big is fencing? 82
Niche sporting in context 84
A balancing act 86
The benefits of community 89
Chapter 8: Fencing Across the USA 93
Mindset of American fencing 94
Club structure in the United States 98
Variety in outlook 99
Chapter 9: The Power of University Training 101
University structure in the United States 103
University fencing = Soviet bloc training 106
Chapter 10: System of Competitions 109
Getting started young 109
U.S. Fencing's competitive hierarchy 112
Special features of the American system 116
Willingness to adapt 120
A broad experience 122
Chapter 11: Building on Success 125
Building by skill, not by the clock 127
Doing away with medal counting 128
Keep the essence, but keep progressing 131
Visionary culture 132

    Growing from within 134
    Good enough can never be good enough 136
Chapter 12: Challenges Ahead.. 139
    Lack of depth 140
    Funding 142
    Complacency 147
Chapter 13: Why American Fencing Matters.................. 149
    Real people... 149
    Positive values and outcomes 151
    A future full of possibilities, rooted in integrity........ 154
    Fencing as an art... 156
Appendix A - USA International Competition Results 159
    Olympic Fencing Country Rankings........................... 159
    Olympic Fencing Medal Detail United States............ 161
    Fencing World Championships Country Rankings.. 165
    United States Junior World Fencing Championship Medals 166
Appendix B - Unified Sports Classification System 169
Appendix C - References 171

Preface

How can we know where we're going if we don't know where we've come from?

A sense of history allows us to better shape the future that we want to see in fencing, and this book seeks to explore the history of why American fencing has grown into what it is today. What I've attempted to do, through research and discussion, is to understand how the explosion of success by United States fencers in the last two decades has come to be. After a century mostly spent on the sidelines, how is it that American fencing has burst onto the scene since the year 2000? It's a burning question that I felt compelled to explore.

Since immigrating to the United States and founding Academy of Fencing Masters in the San Francisco Bay Area, my family has been blessed to enjoy a wonderfully integrated and passionate community of fencers. We see this sport through the lens of families who care about the holistic development of their children, with fencing being a central part of their growth. We have personally watched this sport transform the lives of young and old.

Their constant thirst for knowledge and growth inspires our own.

Everywhere I go, I find myself engaging with people about the role of fencing in their lives and in the lives of the people around them. At one of the Grand Prix at Anaheim, California I talked with a young European fencer about the state of fencing in general. He and I discussed the prospects of various contenders in the international community, and he asserted that the American fencers were among the leaders in the field. For this young man in his twenties, it was just a matter of fact that American fencers are among the leaders in the field. For me, a man with a few more years than that behind me, such a thing seemed jarring. My mind started rewinding through the last few decades, and it became clear that we are living in dramatically different times than we were when I was his age. Having watched the rise of American fencing, it never seemed destined to me as it does to him. In the scope of fencing history, American fencing has only just emerged as a leader. I hope that this trend will continue and that American fencers will keep making those inroads, but for him it was just fact.

This is not only where the subject of the book came from, it's where the title came from as well. These differences in perception between the modern generation of fencers and those who still remember the 80's and 90's, they are a driving force in why American fencing is going where it's going. The movie Cool Runnings became a pop culture touchstone when it came out in 1993, and though it was a lot of fiction it was also a lot of truth and a lot of fun. That notion at the heart of the film of hard work with lots of heart, but not so much a podium finish, that's where American fencing was during those years. It's not where we are today!

It's a generation conversation that I've stumbled into over and over in the last several years, and after seeing this common theme I decided the subject was worth a closer look, a deeper analysis. So, I decided to flesh it out in a book, to explore why American fencing has changed in the last two decades no through the lens of coincidence or as a matter of accident, but for what it is - a change that has come about for many reasons, political and economic, social and cultural. Understanding the why behind America's improved position in fencing isn't just for the sake of an intellectual exercise though, by taking a broader view, we can see where American fencing is going.

Any history or analysis is by definition incomplete, that's a fact that cannot be helped. American fencing is a rich web with many different contributors, and we assure you that none has been left out intentionally. The scope of this book is limited, and we welcome your constructive feedback and discussion once you read it. I wrote this book not to lay down the line as to why this or that is happening, but rather as an act of education and exploration. I am naturally curious, naturally questioning as to why things happen the way that they do. There are always reasons. Just as in a fencing match where each fencer brings the fullness of her or his life experience up to that point onto the strip, and that this life experience then informs how the bout plays out for both fencers, so too does the history of fencing lead us to this point as a sport and then informs how the next era of fencing plays out. Understanding why things are happening the way they are, analyzing it just as I would in a fencing match, that's why I was so driven to write this book.

To learn the information I wanted to write about, I had to go somewhere to find that information. One cannot just pull it out of thin air and expect to get an accurate understanding. In the appendices, you'll find additional resources like medal charts and a list of references that we used to discover the history of fencing in America and that will provide you with further reading should you wish it. If you're like us, then you want to keep learning! The biggest joy of writing this book has been in discovering the history of this sport that we love so dearly.

What it's important for us to communicate as well is that this book is only our perspective, and it is only a snapshot in time. I don't believe myself to be an authoritative expert, only an individual who wanted to know more and also share my own insight. Over the last five years, both my wife Irina and I have been humbled by the interest that we have gotten from our writing online at our company blog. She and I are both grateful to every single person who has taken the time to read our words, and it is that support that buoyed me towards writing this book. Thank you to all who are reading!

Chapter 1: Explosive Beginnings in the New World

Fencing has been in America for longer than you think it has.

Most people think of fencing as having been in the United States only in recent history. That's because it has only been covered in fits and starts in the national media. Nobody knows the names of the athletes, and if you talk to just about anyone in America they'll know almost nothing at all about fencing as a sport. Here it's relegated to pirate movies and snippets during the Olympics. The obvious conclusion would be that fencing has only made slight inroads into America recently. What you might be surprised to know is that fencing has actually held a place in American culture from the very beginning of the country's history.

Fencing has held a place in American culture from the very beginning. Since the days of the first colonies in North America, immigrants have brought with them their passions. Edward Blackwell published the first fencing treatise in America in 1734. He dedicated his pamphlet "To all Gentleman, Promoters, and Lovers of the Art of Fencing in North America." Though his is the first published record of fencing in the New World, it's only the tip of the iceberg.

One of the signers of the Declaration of Independence, Philadelphia physician Dr. Benjamin Rush, believed in fencing as a form of exercise both for the body and the mind. In 1772 he wrote:

"FENCING calls forth most of the muscles into exercise, particularly those which move the limbs. The brain is likewise roused by it, through the avenue of the eyes, and its action, as in the case of music, is propagated to the whole system."

Fencing instructors advertised themselves in large cities like New York and Boston from the earliest days of the United States, as fencing held a high place in society as a mark of refinery and genteelness. Honor and justice maintained a central role in the culture of fencing in America from the very beginning. Fencers practiced in public spaces and private rooms until the first fencing school in America opened in 1754 in New York, under the tutelage of an immigrant from Holland named John Rievers. Other fencing instructors hailing from France, England, Italy and more followed suit in the years that followed. With names like Saint Pry, Du Poke, William

Turner, Thomas Varin, and Peter Vianni, fencing masters came to America and fostered the early development of American fencing. It's notable that most fencing schools of this era were part of wider schools that taught dance, music, poetry, etc. It's also notable that fencing schools stretched up and down the colonies, reaching all the way down into the South to Charleston, which was home to several fencing schools prior to the American Revolution.

Still, when George Washington initially led the country against Britain in the American Revolution he did so with a musket, not a fencing sword. Private duels of that period, like the famous showdown between Alexander Hamilton and Aaron Burr, were fought with guns, not with swords. In the lead up to the American Revolution, fencing masters in the American did train "gentleman soldiers" in the art of sword work. When muskets ran out of ammunition, military men learned to rely on whatever skills they had at their disposal. Though fencing had already crossed into the realm of sport during times of peace in Europe, during times of war it found a place in the virulence of soldiers in the American Revolution.

Fencing originally came to America as an antidote to gun violence, with proponents of the sport heralding it as a means to draw down violent tendencies rather than inflaming them. During and after the American Revolution it became a bloody testament to the power of the sword. Following the American Revolution and through the American Civil War, which ended on May 9, 1865, fencing training veered further towards fighting and further from sport fencing. Especially in the southern United States, sword duels rose in popularity. In the north, fencing exhibitions didn't end in death, but they did run until one fencer drew blood from his opponent.

Sport fencing had been on the rise in Europe for some time, however it wasn't until the late 19th century that American fencing turned from blood to sport. Keep in mind, American shores held two nationwide wars in the span of a half century. Fighting couldn't be play during these times because lives were at stake.

Even in the early days of fencing, we see the mark of the melting pot on the style of fencing in America. Fencers could train with a wide variety of masters from all over the world at American fencing schools from the inception of the United States. *American exceptionalism* is the notion that American is unique. Unlike any other country on Earth, America is a country that is not bound by traditions that reach back into a history beyond our comprehension. It is a country built by the people and for the people, where individuals are free to create the world that they want to see. The mission of the United States centers on individualistic pursuits and the push for greatness. Americans always want to be more than they are today, to be the best. In some places that's seen negatively as bravado, but the positive spin on it is that American culture fosters competition and individualism. Those last two concepts are central to sport fencing. The history of fencing in America is tightly tied to the revolutionary fighting spirit of American culture.

While in Europe fencing had begun to emerge as a sport as far back as the 18th century, in America it remained very much a weapon. It wasn't until the United States had moved on from war to restoration that finally the sword was sheathed, and fencing became a sport instead of a means of bloodshed. In 1891, the Amateur Fencing League of America, a group which would later become our modern United States Fencing Association (USFA) or as they call it now USA Fencing, was formed in New York to govern sport fencing in America. When you realize that only thirty years prior to the Civil War had engulfed the country, the rise of sport fencing could easily be seen as an outgrowth of the necessarily ingrained military culture in the United States.

In fencing, the American melting pot has from the beginning created a culture in the sport that is wholly different from the fencing cultures of other countries. Without the codified fencing schools that existed in Europe, fencers in America have been free to create a fencing style that is their own. America's unique path in fencing, wholly different from its development in other countries, is part of why fencing took so long to take root here in comparison. It's notable to realize that American fencers had some positive results at the end of the 19th century and beginning of the 20th century, just as the Olympics began to shape the sport. Fencers Albertson Van Zo Post and Charles Tatham took the silver and bronze that the St. Louis Olympics in 1904 in both epee and foil (yes, the same medals in two events), with the American foil team taking the silver at those same games. William Grebe and Albertson Van Zo Post took silver and bronze in saber as well. We should note that the competition in those games were totally dominated by American athletes because really, no one else joined in the competition. Four out of five athletes were American at the Olympics in St. Louis. It was a different Olympics than what we know, one that would be frankly very weird to us today.

Though there is this arguably rich and complex history of the sport in the United States early on, America put little to no emphasis on fencing for more than a half century following the start of the Olympic Games in 1896. The Soviet Union on the other hand put a great deal of effort into reinventing the sport and thus their fencers rose to dominance in the world scene while America lagged behind in skill and organization through the mid Twentieth century. What's fascinating is how those same drives and desires of American exceptionalism, the ones that wound their way through war and revolution, remain at the heart of American fencing over one hundred years on.

Chapter 2: Extreme underdogs

Once fencing became codified as a sport with the Olympic Games, the sport took the international stage in a big way. As one of the founding ten events, fencing has a history that you can't separate from the Olympics.

Americans were part of fencing from the early days, with the United States medaling all the way back in the 1904 Olympic Games in team foil, individual foil, epee, sabre, and stick fencing. It's important to notice that only three countries participated in these Olympics in St. Louis, Missouri. Germany, Cuba, and the United States dominated the medals because they were the only fencers competing! Those first few Olympic Games weren't close to what we see today, with epic events that dozens of countries vie for.

It would be nearly two decades before America would get to the Olympic podium again in fencing. Even then, the United States medaled only here and there, and not with gold for a century. In fact, through more than a century of Olympic fencing, the United States has only won a single gold medal in men's fencing and only two gold medals in women's fencing! It's interesting and important to know that those two gold medals for American women came in the 2004 and 2008 while that men's gold came in the 1904 games that were barely attended by other countries at all. There were exactly one hundred years between American fencers winning Olympic gold.

During the years in between, there's no doubt that Americans were extreme underdogs. Below are the rankings for Olympic Fencing, from the beginning of the Games to the most recent. You'll notice that women's fencing doesn't start until 1924; that's because women's events were not included until the eighth Olympiad in Paris. What you'll notice here is that the United States is truly low in the pack, 10th in women's fencing in gold medals and 16th in men's fencing in gold medals. The overall medal count is somewhat better, with the men tied for fifth with Poland and the women tied for eighth with China.

More significant than the rankings are the raw numbers. For instance, look a fencing powerhouse Italy. Italian fencers hold 27 women's fencing medals and 96 men's fencing medals, for a total of 123. France is a bit behind with 12 women's fencing medals and 103 men's fencing medals, making it total 115 Olympic fencing medals. The United States isn't even in the ballpark, with our total at 28. The Soviet Union hasn't even existed as a fencing competitor in nearly thirty years, and it stopped competing as a country almost three decades ago, yet they're still ahead of the United States with 49 overall medals. If Americans got just one fencer on the podium in every fencing event, there is the potential for eighteen medals across the sport at each Olympiad between the men and the women's teams now that all events are included in the Games. It would still take us more than two decades to even catch up to France, and that's assuming they didn't win a single medal.

Of course, this snapshot only tells a small portion of the story, but it is nonetheless emblematic of where America stands in Olympic fencing. American fencing has made a total turnaround. Here are the total medal counts for the Olympics, through the 2016 Games. I've put them here so that you can get a full picture of the numbers but know that we're going to blow these charts apart later in this chapter.

Olympic Women's Fencing Country Rankings 1924-2016					
Rank	Country	Gold	Silver	Bronze	Total
1	Italy	11	8	8	27
2	Hungary	8	6	7	21
3	Russia	6	3	2	11
4	Soviet Union	5	3	2	10
5	France	4	3	5	12
6	West Germany	3	2	1	6
7	Germany	2	5	3	10
8	Romania	2	4	4	10
9	China	2	4	3	9
10	United States	2	2	5	9

Olympic Men's Fencing Country Rankings 1896-2016					
Rank	Country	Gold	Silver	Bronze	Total
1	France	37	37	29	103
2	Italy	37	34	25	96
3	Hungary	29	17	20	66
4	Soviet Union	13	12	14	39
5	Cuba	6	5	6	17
6	Russia	6	2	5	13
7	Poland	4	8	7	19
8	West Germany	4	6	0	10
9	Belgium	3	3	4	10
10	Germany	3	2	6	11
11	Sweden	2	3	2	7
12	China	2	3	0	5
13	Romania	2	1	3	6

14	Greece	2	1	1	4
15	South Korea	2	0	3	5
16	United States	1	7	11	19

American fencing sputters

Growth for American fencing has come slow, in fits and in starts. Unlike the powerhouse teams of Europe and Asia, American fencers have had to work largely independently of government support or long-standing fencing clubs. Without a central force to drive fencing in America, the sport has struggled to foster the kind of athletes that can compete on the world and Olympic stages.

This is particularly true of mid-century fencing in the United States. During the heat of the Cold War in the 1960's and 1970's, national sports served as proxies for world superpowers. We saw this most in sports like hockey, figure skating and gymnastics, where the United States competed against the Soviet Union. While these two countries fought against each other for dominance in the political world, their athletes fought against each other for dominance on the podium. However in fencing we didn't see this. American fencing never challenged the Soviet bloc of countries like Poland, Hungary, Romania, Cuba, and the Soviet Union itself for fencing dominance in the middle of the Twentieth Century. American fencing saw only a handful of podium finishes throughout the Cold War.

Every individual athlete has their own reasons to push themselves to succeed in their sport and drive their life towards high level competitions like the Olympic Games, the World Championships, etc., but we see many of those reasons again and again. On the world stage, athletes are not just competing for themselves, they're competing for their country as well. When you stand for your nation, it's different than when you compete for yourself. There is a sense of national pride, a sense of deep responsibility that an athlete feels. It's for you, and it's for your family, but it's for your people as well. It's meaningful to be a part of something bigger, to have a place of honor in your social group. Extend that from a small group to your whole country, and it's a feeling beyond glory. You know that if you win, it'll be because of you that those numbers in the charts point in a different direction, towards your nation. That was especially true during the Cold War. Every matchup became bigger, not just about one fencer winning against another. As the two sides were pushing against one another, the matchups took on the epic proportion of being about good versus evil at times, an extension of the Cold War. Fencing never took on the importance of rivalries like ice hockey, basketball, or gymnastics during the Cold War, but that was not for a lack of effort.

The primary rivalry in fencing for the second half of the century lie between the old guard fencing schools of Italy and France and the Eastern European nations propelled forward by the Soviet Union. During these years, American fencing stood in disarray. Unlike rival teams abroad, American fencers didn't have training together. Fencers on the West Coast trained on the West Coast. Fencers on the East Coast trained on the East Coast. To be clear, international sports in the United States are all this way. Athletes across the board who train for the Olympic Games or for international competition do so with little to no funding from the government even today. Getting to the international stage for most American athletes is as much about getting the money to train as it is about training itself. For athletes from the Soviet bloc, this was exactly the opposite. The governments of these countries not only paid for training, they also hired the best coaches and sought out the best athletes to groom for success.

The result has been that American fencing has had to think on its feet, feeling its way through to some success instead of having a unifying guide. Individual fencers blazed their way to the podium doing whatever they could. Without a legacy of accomplished coaches to train them, the road has been bumpy.

Let's look at this another way. Here is the Olympic fencing medal count for the United States since 1908, broken at the year 2000.

- U.S. Olympic Fencing Medals 1908-1999, 20 Olympic Games, 91 years
    - Men, 8
    - Women, 0
- U.S. Olympic Fencing Medals 2000-2016, 5 Olympic Games, 16 years
    - Men, 4
    - Women, 9

Over the course of ninety-one years, American male fencers won just eight medals. That's one medal every 11.375 years. In other words, it is only one medal in 4 consecutive Olympic Games! In the first sixteen years of the Twentieth Century they earned four medals, or one medal every 4 years or looking at this differently, one medal in each Olympic Games. At this rate, American men will have twenty medals in the same number of games! The women have shown a much more dramatic growth. Prior to the year 2000, American women had never won a medal. In the first four Olympics of the 21st Century, American women won nine Olympic medals! It's a massive change, and one that we cannot ignore.

Hiccups in the making a mark

What American fencers did have throughout the middle of the twentieth century was grit and determination. We saw many fencers work hard to train and prepare for the international competitions, qualify for them, and then fail to make their mark.

Again and again in the Olympic Games we saw American fencers fail to progress through the initial rounds and onto the final series of bouts. Both individually and in the team events, American fencers have historically found themselves eliminated early on, well before the medal bouts. First round losses have been unfortunately common for American fencers, and second round eliminations have proven to be equally frustrating. Great American fencers like foilist Albert Axelrod and Peter Westbrook were able to break through to the final rounds, but these were phenomenal examples amongst decades of international competition. Axelrod, who won bronze in the 1960 Olympic Games, was the first American foilist to advance to the finals in a Fencing World Championship until Gerek Meinhardt repeated that feat half-century later, in 2010. It's notable that Axelrod was the son of Russian Jewish immigrants, a mirror of the influence of Russian culture on American fencing that would come to be nearly a half century after he took the Olympic podium.

The drought in Olympic medals in fencing lasted from 1932 to 1960, then again from 1960 to 1984. American fencers struggled to make headway. It wasn't just the Olympics though. American fencing struggled on the broader international stage at the World Championships as well. This is a pattern that we see emerge across competitions and across weapons. From the mid-century onward, American fencing is nowhere near the level that other countries maintained consistently.

While the Olympics are something unique in sports, the United States performance on the world stage follows a similar path through the Fencing World Championships. This annual competition has been going on in some form since 1921 and is organized by the Fédération Internationale d'Escrime or FIE (in English - International Fencing Federation), the governing body of the international fencing. It's the most prominent fencing competition in the world behind the Olympics, but since it takes place every year rather than every four years the dynamics are quite different.

Some things do stay the same between the two. Once again we see Italy, Hungary, the Soviet Union, and France as massively dominant in the medal count. The United States has less than ten percent of the number of medals that Italy has in the Fencing World Championships. Ten percent! It's an extraordinary number. The United States has in fact won fewer medals in the Fencing World Championships than in the Olympics, despite there being almost four times as many opportunities to do so. Also of note here is that nearly twenty percent (six) of the medals in this medal count were won in the Fencing World Championships in 2018. Prior to this year, the United States had won only 25 medals.

Fencing World Championships Country Rankings 1937-2018					
Rank	Country	Gold	Silver	Bronze	Total
1	Italy	118	102	124	344
2	Hungary	90	84	94	268
3	Soviet Union	90	57	50	197
4	France	89	97	95	281
5	Russia	53	26	37	116
6	West Germany	25	26	14	65
7	Germany	22	29	39	90
8	Poland	17	29	39	85
9	Romania	13	25	28	66
10	Ukraine	11	11	15	37
11	United States	9	12	10	31
12	China	7	18	17	42

13	Sweden	7	13	17	37
14	South Korea	6	11	19	36
15	Cuba	6	5	9	20

What's clear from both the Olympics and the Fencing World Championships is that American fencing has a long way to go to even be in the same league as the dominant fencing countries.

Throughout this time period, the American system of training its fencers proved to fail both spectacularly and in the closeness of competition. Where fencers from those dominant countries had a support system to bolster their efforts, American fencing simply did not. No unified training meant that individual fencers learned the ropes, but that knowledge did not make it down to the next generation of fencers in the same way it did with European countries that dominated the sport. Think of it as though the American fencers were running an individual race where those in other countries were running it as a relay. At some point the individual can't keep going. Successful fencing countries were passing the baton from one to another, gaining momentum and knowledge with every pass. America on the other hand simply started again with each fencer. It's simply impossible to get ahead this way, no matter how much grit and determination you may have.

Chapter 3: Close but Not Quite

Things began taking a turn for the better in American fencing in the 1980's.

After decades of Soviet domination in international fencing, the 1984 Olympic Games in Los Angeles were boycotted by fourteen Eastern Bloc countries. This followed the American-led boycott of the 1980 Games in Moscow, where sixty-six countries didn't participate in the Olympics. In terms of American fencing, the 1984 boycott meant that those Soviet sphere nations got out of the way of the podium. In men's individual sabre, France took gold, Italy took silver, and the United States took bronze as Peter Westbrook became the first American to get to the podium in more than two decades.

The changing face of American fencing

While politics certainly played into the ability of America to get that Olympic medal in 1984, it's still true that America's fencing took a major turn in the right direction in the eighties and nineties. Peter Westbrook's talent and hard work won him that medal, but one aspect that made him so different was the legacy that he took part in. Though he didn't benefit from being part of a long line of competitive fencers per se, Westbrook has a uniquely American road to his fencing dominance that does include legacy.

Westbrook's maternal uncle was a famous Japanese kendo master, kendo being a traditional Japanese style of wooden sword fencing. It was at the urging of his mother that he began training in fencing as a child, in large part because of his heritage. Once he became serious about the sport and chose sabre as his weapon, Westbrook sought out a mentor to coach him. He found one in Hungarian fencing master and immigrant Csaba Elthes, who would go on to coach Westbrook through his Olympic career and beyond. In general, sabre fencing, both women's and men's, reached much higher level and got there faster than other weapons. Hungarian coaches like Elthes were particularly important in shaping the coaching culture. After fleeing the political strife in Hungary in 1956, Elthes saw an opportunity for sabre fencing in the United States and settled in New York, where he and fellow Hungarian immigrant maestro Giorgio Santelli were among the driving forces behind American sabre fencing. Santelli was the son of Italo Santelli, the "Father of Modern Sabre Fencing." Elthes and other immigrant fencing instructors in New York City created a fertile soil for American fencing to take root. His focus on the intellectual aspects of fencing as opposed to physical acuity continues to influence the American spirit of fencing.

With this kind of top-level coaching, Westbrook's record in fencing is unmatched even twenty-five years after his Olympic win. He won the United States Individual Sabre title thirteen times between 1974 and 1995, and in 1995 at the age of forty-two he won gold at the Pan American Games.

In Peter Westbrook we can see how American fencing began to build a legacy, one rooted in a totally different strategy than that of European and Asian fencing. It's a legacy that he's used to leverage for the future of fencing, one that we'll discuss later.

It's not just the competitive men of the era that shaped fencing going forward. Stacey Johnson, a member of the 1980 U.S. Olympic team that didn't compete, went on to become the first woman to serve a full term as USFA president (USFA is short for the United States Fencing Association, a US governing body of the Olympic Sport of Fencing). Not only that, but she served as the president of FIE Women in Fencing Council in 2012 and continues her tenure until 2020. Johnson was instrumental in getting women's sabre added to the 2004 Olympic Games. Her years as a world class fencer and top-level collegiate fencer in the 1970's and 1980's deeply contributed to her ability to lead and be a part of the success of American fencing years later.

Fueled by European fencing masters

Multiple American fencers from the 1960s, the 1970s, and 1980s would go on to become successful coaches here in the States. It turns out that this time period in American fencing was instrumental in laying the foundation for the future of the sport, creating that generational knowledge that is necessary for success at the international level.

Throughout this time period, renowned fencing masters immigrated from Europe to make their home in the United States. Fencers from France, Hungary, and Poland established a major presence here, implementing the training styles here that had brought them such success in Europe. The discipline and instinctive competitive nature of European fencing became embedded in the schools that these coaches founded.

This manifested in a few clusters around New York City, Portland, Seattle, and the San Francisco Bay Area.

New York City has a history of fencing dating back to at least 1850, but what's most interesting is that some estimates put upwards of eighty percent of American Olympic fencers coming out of New York. For a long time, NYC was the center of American fencing. Everything started from here, going all the way back to long before there was a twinkle of fencing spread anywhere else. The majority of national champions and team members across the history of American fencing have come from here. Its clubs have the richest traditions and the longest histories. The Fencers Club in New York City is the oldest fencing club in the country, and it has a huge heritage in U.S. fencing. European immigrants drove that initial spark and continue to drive the growth of the sport. The list of coaches and national champions from New York goes on for miles, and this area is also brimming with smaller fencing clubs and programs. It's a community of fencing, and much of the growth and forward motion that's come from this area has to do with the booming immigrant population in the city that brought fencing coaches and fencers here from Europe.

Colleen Olney, the "Mother of Oregon Fencing", was the first coach of her sons Robert and Michael Marx, who each competed in multiple Olympic Games. She would later become founding member of the club that spawned fencing champion Mariel Zagunis. A competitor in her own right, Olney fenced competitively in the 1960s but wanted to create a rich fencing environment for her sons. To that end, she brought masters Yves Auriol and Alex Beguinet from France to teach her fencers in the 1970s, and much later Ed Korfanty from Poland to foster the surge of champions that we saw in the early 2000s. These European fencing masters contributed to explosion of American fencing during this time period and the legacy that it left. Olney's own legacy exists not only in her sons, but also in the Northwest Fencing Center, Oregon Fencing Alliance, which are some top fencing clubs in the country, and successful longstanding free fencing programs in the Portland area. Her son Michael would go on to found a stalwart fencing club of his own on the other side of the country in Massachusetts.

San Francisco is another hotbed of fencing training in the United States, and it's home to some of the oldest clubs in the country. Once again, we see the European influence in the Bay Area, as many of the schools were founded by fencing champions from Europe. The first of these came from Olympian Hans Halberstadt, who survived the Holocaust due to his rescue from Dachau through fencing connections and then came to San Francisco where he built a new fencing life. He trained German fencing champion Helene Mayer, and the school bearing his name that was founded in 1968 has proven to be fertile ground for American coaches to develop their skills, including Greg Massialas, Michael D'Asaro, Peter Burchard, and more. Massialas founded and coaches at the Massialas Foundation (MTEAM Fencing) in San Francisco, in addition to coaching the USA National Men's Foil Team.

One beautiful thing about America is that there is diversity in fencing geography. While NYC, Seattle, and San Francisco are centers of American fencing, there are outlier powerhouses as well that drew European fencing masters. Three-time Olympic gold medalist Vladimir Nazlymov immigrated to the U.S. when the Soviet flag came down, landing at the Ohio State University where he led teams at the USA World Championship and the World University Games. While Nazlymov was a prominent Soviet fencer bringing his talent to the United States, he's hardly the only one to jump the pond. George Pogosov for one, who is an Olympic gold medalist in the 1992 Olympics, he was born in Kiev, Ukraine and is now the head coach at Stanford University. In the wake of the fall of the Soviet Union, a whole slew of fencing coaches and former champions came to the United States, helping to fuel the pool of talent that would train the fencers to come.

The importance of almost

While the fencers of the last two decades of the twentieth century didn't see the explosive results that they would have perhaps like to have seen, they are a critical part of the story of the rise of American fencing. They almost got to the top of that Olympic podium. They almost made those international Olympic dreams come true.

Of the entirety of the history of American fencing, this time period is one of the most important. Without the knowledge that the top competitive American fencers created during these decades, there would be no future success at all. In the fencing schools of Europe, the skills were part of a tutelage that came down over centuries. In the Soviet bloc, those same skills were honed in structured training fueled by national politics. In America, the indomitable spirit of progress kept fencers working hard to crack the code and reach the top. The last bit of learning took a great deal of time and effort on the part of American fencers, much of it trial and error. Without that trial and error there couldn't be the coaching to propel later American fencers forward.

Fencing in the United States almost reached world championship level. These fencers almost got there! But when they didn't make it, they didn't leave fencing. They went on to support the sport in other ways, throwing their passion in for the athletes that would follow. Through coaching and administration, the athletes of the eighties and nineties became a linchpin in the story of American fencing.

Greatness doesn't happen in one fell swoop. What happened for U.S. fencing in the eighties and nineties proved to be a taste of the success that would come with the next generation of fencers. It's truly a case of American fencers reaching toward that greatness but just not quite having the tools to get there. Without this period there wouldn't be enough of a foundation to build on for the future of the sport.

Chapter 4: Tide turns in the 2000s

There are moments in life when it's possible to feel the ground shift from one direction to another. Old ways of life, ways that seemed like they could never change are suddenly different. At the turn of the millennium, American fencing felt one of those shifts.

What follows are details of how the United States made an explosive and lasting mark on the world fencing scene. The seismic shift is impossible to ignore, and breathtaking in its stamina. After a century of dominance by Old World and Soviet bloc fencing schools, it's almost as if the Americans finally woke up and started fencing!

America flips the switch on the World Championship

What's truly fascinating about this time period is how it seems that American fencing just flipped a switch. Prior to the year 2000, no American fencing team or individual, in epee, foil, or sabre, whether a man or a woman, had won a gold medal at the World

Championship or at the Junior World Championship. That's absolutely zero. Then suddenly we see the United States consistently challenging for and making it to the top of the podium.

The chart below details the Fencing World Championship Gold medals. Notice that this chart starts with the 2000 Fencing World Championships. That's because no fencer from the United States had won prior to that date. We see that the movement in American fencing starts with a thrust of young cadet/junior female fencers coming onto the scene. It was the women fencers who first made it to the top of the podium, not men, both in teams and individually. The men's first junior gold individual medal came only in 2013 through Alexander Massialas. Compare this to ladies, who had long made it to the top of the Olympic podium by then. In fact, by that time in every individual discipline, foil, sabre and epee, there were American women who took the gold at the Junior World Junior Championships.

The first American to win a World Championship in any age category, any weapon, was a then fourteen-year-old foilist, Iris Zimmermann, when she won the Cadet World Championship Gold medal in 1995. Impressive for any fencer, but all the more for her age. She's believed to be the youngest fencer ever to win a World Championship, besides being the first American. The experience for her was overwhelming, but also spurred her on to compete in the individual and team foil events in the 2000 Summer Olympics. She also competed and won at the Junior World Championships in 2000, again becoming the first American to conquer this title. Moreover, she won bronze at the Senior World Championships in 1999, again becoming a first American women fencer to win a medal at the senior worlds.

Iris is a member of the US Fencing Hall of Fame. Her older sister, Felicia Zimmermann, is an impressive foilist as well, but was the first and only woman to win NCAA championships in epee and foil. Felicia and Iris competed alongside each other in individual and team foil at the 2000 Olympics. The two bought the renowned Rochester Fencing Club in 2009, where they now coach fencing champions.

Now we come back to that idea of American fencing building through in a generational way. Mariel Zagunis, now the most decorated American fencer in history and the woman who led that 2000 Women's Sabre team, came through the same school that Olympians Michael and Robert Marx came through. Remember that it was

Marx's mother Collen Olney who became an integral part of the fencing community there in support of her sons. Zagunis's coach Ed Korfanty was in fact recruited by Olney to train Robert and Michael. He then took on the role of fostering sabre only, and those results are obviously astounding as his fencers went on to incredible success.

One thing to take note of with regard to the Fencing World Championship is that women's sabre fencing was only added to the competition in 1999. It's also worth knowing that the first Fencing World Championship was held in 1921. That means it took almost eighty years for an American to get to the top of the podium. The consistent preparation of young talent at the Cadet/Junior level in youth fencing is an absolute requirement for fencing to succeed on the senior level since this gives a firm foundation of experience, confidence, and hope.

Fencing World Championship Gold - American Winner	
2000	Women's Team Sabre
2005	Women's Team Sabre
2006	Women's Individual Sabre - Rebecca Ward
2009	Women's Individual Sabre - Mariel Zagunis
2010	Women's Individual Sabre - Mariel Zagunis
2012	Men's Team Epee
2013	Men's Individual Foil - Miles Chamley-Watson
2018	Women's Team Foil, Women's Team Epee

If the Fencing World Championship gold medal count is impressive, it's nothing compared to what happened for America at the Junior World Fencing Championship. As in the World Fencing Championship, Americans did not hold a single title prior to the year 2000.

Why is America so much more dominant in the Junior World Fencing Championship than in the World Fencing Championship? The simple answer is age. The Junior World Fencing Championship accepts fencers up to the age of twenty. Remember that the American fencing program is growing, it's at its beginning. That means that these are the younger fencers who have had the benefit of the legacy built by previous generations of fencers. At the Junior age, fencers have their whole support either from clubs and their families, or from universities and the NCAA programs. Later on, it will become more challenging to get that support. This is the reason a great many fencers drop from serious competitiveness and instead focus on their careers outside of fencing.

The legacy aspect here is a key factor. Without the expertise that has been handed down from one generation of Olympic fencers to another, the American fencing team would not be making these incredible strides. That's true in some part for nearly every fencer who rose to the top.

It's notable how massive this chart for the Junior World Fencing Championship is. This competition was first held in 1950, but there was not a single American gold medal until the year 2000.

Junior World Fencing Championship	
2000	Women's Individual Foil - Iris Zimmerman
2001	Women's Team Sabre
2001	Men's Team Sabre
2001	Women's Individual Sabre - Mariel Zagunis
2003	Women's Individual Sabre - Sada Jacobson
2004	Women's Individual Sabre - Sada Jacobson
2004	Women's Team Sabre
2005	Women's Individual Sabre - Mariel Zagunis
2005	Women's Team Sabre
2005	Men's Team Sabre
2005	Women's Individual Foil - Emily Cross
2006	Women's Individual Sabre - Mariel Zagunis
2006	Women's Team Sabre
2006	Men's Team Sabre
2006	Women's Individual Foil - Emily Cross

2008	Men's Team Foil
2009	Women's Individual Epee - Kelley Hurley
2009	Women's Team Epee
2010	Men's Team Foil
2011	Men's Team Foil
2011	Women's Individual Foil Nzingha Prescod
2012	Men's Team Foil
2013	Men's Individual Foil Alexander Massialas
2013	Women's Team Sabre
2014	Women's Individual Foil - Lee Kiefer
2015	Women's Individual Foil - Sara Taffel
2015	Women's Team Foil
2015	Men's Individual Sabre - Eli Dershwitz
2016	Women's Individual Foil - Sabrina Massialas
2017	Men's Team Foil
2018	Women's Team Foil

| 2018 | Men's Individual Foil - Nick Itkin |
| 2019 | Women's Individual Foil – Lauren Scruggs |

Challenging at the Olympics

The shift didn't happen only at the World Championship level but followed through to the Olympic level. American fencers went from nearly nothing to consistent challengers in the Olympics starting in 2004. Again, this transformation is absolutely stunning.

Take women's fencing. Prior to the 2004 Olympic Games in Athens, American women's fencing was dead last in the medal count. No woman had ever brought home a single medal for the United States. Mariel Zagunis and Sada Jacobson took the gold and bronze in the inaugural women's individual sabre event. Note here that women's sabre was not included in the Olympic Games until Athens. What an incredible way for it to start!

Following the women's success in Athens, American women fencers went on to go from last place in the Olympic medal count to the top ten in just a dozen years.

It's a remarkable transformation, one unlike anything else in the history of modern sport fencing.

American men have had an explosive rise in Olympic fencing in the last twenty years as well, though not to the level of the women. No male American fencer had made it to the Olympic podium since Peter Westbrook in 1984. That changed in Beijing in 2008 when the men's sabre team took home silver. American men would go on to win silver in individual foil in 2016 in Rio with Alexander Massialas's performance and that same year to win bronze in the men's team foil. Not only that, but Daryl Homer took home silver in men's individual sabre in Rio as well. That's four Olympic medals in eight years, more than the American men had earned in the prior seventy years.

Here's a full breakdown of women and men's fencing results in the Olympic Games from 2004-2016. The last column includes details about which rival countries also made it to the podium during each Olympiad.

2004 Athens			
Women's Individual Sabre	Gold	Mariel Zagunis	Silver - China
Women's Individual Sabre	Bronze	Sada Jacobson	
2008 Beijing			
Women's Individual Sabre	Gold	Mariel Zagunis	
Women's Individual Sabre	Silver	Sada Jacobson	
Women's Individual Sabre	Bronze	Rebecca Ward	
Women's Team Sabre	Bronze	Mariel Zagunis, Sada Jacobson, Rebecca Ward	Gold – Ukraine; Silver - China

Women's Team Foil	Silver	Erinn Smart, Hanna Thompson, Emily Cross	Gold - Russia; Bronze - Italy
Men's Team Sabre	Silver	Tim Morehouse, Jason Rogers, Keeth Smart, James Williams	Gold - South Korea Bronze - Italy
2012 London			
Women's Team Epee	Bronze	Courtney Hurley, Kelley Hurley, Maya Lawrence, Susie Scanlan	Gold - China Silver - South Korea
2016 Rio			
Women's Team Sabre	Bronze	Ibtihaj Muhammad, Dagmara Wozniak, Mariel Zagunis, Monica Aksamit	Gold - Russia; Silver - Ukraine

Men's Individual Foil	Silver	Alexander Massialas	Gold - Italy; Bronze - Russia
Men's Team Foil	Bronze	Miles Chamley-Watson, Race Imboden, Alexander Massialas, Gerek Meinhardt	Gold - Russia; Silver - France
Men's Individual Sabre	Silver	Daryl Homer	Gold - Hungary Bronze - South Korea

Notice that last column here. Those dominant fencers from the former Soviet bloc countries and from the European powerhouses of fencing haven't gone anywhere. We still see them challenging for and winning top spots on the Olympic podium through the last twenty years. Hungary, Russia, South Korea, China, and the Ukraine are all continuing to be highly competitive and highly successful. Italy and France, those old-world members of the fencing elite, are also continuing to claim their place on the Olympic stage. Note that this chart is skewed slightly because we have only included those disciplines where U.S. teams/fencers medaled. If we were to include all events, Italy and France would dominate. To keep the focus of this book narrow, we've kept our medal charts sparse.

Coming into our own

American fencers are far from dominating the international stage completely, but there's no doubt that they are in the conversation now. Where just a few years ago it would have been ridiculous to imagine multiple American fencers in the top ranks at the World Fencing Championship or at the Olympic Games, now it's not unusual to see Americans at those top spots.

This is such a dramatic change that it's simply impossible not to marvel at it. What's surprising and heartening here is that this isn't just one fencing school, it's many fencing schools across the United States who are creating their own melting pot of fencing success. The twenty-first century has proven to be the moment when American fencing comes into its own.

While the Americans might have stormed onto the world stage in a big way, through nearly twenty years of competition with dozens of athletes, it's clear that this success is no fluke but rather the culmination of many factors finally coming together. Understanding why and how those factors came together is an important part of helping American fencing to continue to grow and prosper.

Recent History's Huge Successes

The rise of American fencing continues to grow over the last year, building towards the 2020 Olympics in Tokyo. For the first time, in every gender/weapon/age category American fencers are seeing consistent seeding at the top of the world fencing rankings.

2018 brought two male foilists, Race Imboden and Alexander Massialas, to the number one and number two spots in FIE's world ranking. That's unprecedented in the history of this sport. Female foilists from the U.S. are pushing towards the top as well, with Lee Kiefer in the top three for women. Eli Derschwitz sits in the top three in world rankings for men's sabre as well. He finished the 2018 season as number one in the world.

That's not to say anything of the dozen other American fencers in the top sixteen across epee, foil, and sabre in the international rankings for 2018 thus far.

Let's also summarize the end of 2017-2018 season, which culminated in Senior World Championship in Wuxi, China but looking at the top 16 in the world rankings at that time, since these are considered to be the top ranked fencers in the world.

- Women's Epee - Courtney Hurley (10)
- Women's Foil - Keifer (3), Ross (11), Prescod (13)
- Women's Sabre - Wozniak (9), Stone (13). It's notable that Zagunis is also climbing back from her maternity leave from the sport to try for her fifth Olympics in Tokyo.
- Men's Epee - McDowald (9)
- Men's Foil - Imboden (3), Massialas (8), Meinhard (15)
- Men's Sabre - Derschwitz (1), Homer (15)

It is not unusual that during the season American fencers make the top of the ranking, with Keifer, Imboden, Meinhard, and Massialas being a great example of such. This many fencers being so near the top is progress over the past. Not only that, but the team improvement in ranking is impressive.

- Women's Epee - USA (1)
- Women's Foil - USA (3)
- Women's Sabre - USA (5)
- Men's Foil - USA (1)
- Men's Epee - USA (7)
- Men's Sabre - USA (7)

Similar rankings among the Juniors back up the observation that this is not just a fluke, but a pattern of high rankings.

Whereas the past had American fencers going to the top of the international fencing world in fits and starts, with single fencers making it to the top once in a few dozen years, today's landscape is completely different. It is unquestionable that the United States is now on par with powerhouse fencing countries around the world. It's all right there in the rankings. What's most important in this story is the consistency with which American fencers have been challenging for the top positions. We can now look back over more than a decade of American fencers performing in the highest echelons of the sport.

It's worth reiterating the statics for American fencing since the year 2000.

- 33 Junior World Fencing Championship Gold Medals
- 7 Fencing World Championship Gold Medals
- 13 Olympic Medals

Note that these don't include Grand Prix or World Cups competitions. Those outcomes tell much the same story, with American fencers seemingly coming out of nowhere in the last twenty years after having small showings for a century.

The numbers are truly a marvel. Each one of those numbers represents the culmination of years of hard work, dedication, and inspired coaching. This kind of success doesn't happen overnight, not in the slightest. Though it may seem like American fencing just fell into the international world in the new millennium, there's a bigger story here, one that can be traced across the country and across continents.

Chapter 5: Fall of the Soviet Union

It may seem like international politics are very far away from us. How can something that happens on the other side of the world affect your life in a meaningful way? It turns out that the world is a much smaller place than it feels.

Before we can explore how the fall of the Soviet Union affected American fencing, we first have to understand what made the USSR able to dominate to begin with.

We also do want to take a moment to note that none of this analysis is meant to slight the hard work and dedication of the fencers who hailed from the Soviet bloc in any way. One of the most beautiful things about sport in general and about fencing in particular is that it brings us together. Respect for the opponent and the value that they bring to this experience is central, even as we pick apart the history of our sport.

The Soviet Republic

During the Cold War, the United States and the Soviet Union seemed to be on opposite sides of everything. Funnily enough, the walls between the two superpowers actually bound the two together inextricably. As each one worked to outdo the other, the ambition of each became more prominent. The USSR and America fought fiercely for world dominance after being allies during WWII. That rivalry extended to economic matters, military matters, and notably to sports. These two nations essentially fought proxy wars against one another via their athletes on the world stage.

Representing your country on the international stage as an athlete is significant no matter the context. There is a sense of pride that goes beyond just competing in a sport, because you are not only there for yourself but for all the people in your country. It's monumental, meaningful. During the time of the Cold War, there was an additional feeling of responsibility for athletes on both sides to rise to the occasion as well.

A bit of a history and civics lesson here. The Soviet Union and the United States fundamentally had different philosophies. Where the USSR governed itself with a one party, totalitarian, communist system of government, the U.S. was founded on the idea of a democratic government system with multiple political parties vying for power and based on the free market (obviously this is a constant work in progress). That philosophy of government extended to everything for each country, from the way people got their food to the way athletes trained for the Olympic Games.

Soviet influence reached well beyond the borders of the USSR. The United States and the Soviet Union both had other, smaller countries within their sphere of influence. What that means for fencing is that countries within the Soviet sphere, known as the Eastern bloc, often used similar training and therefore got similar results. Places like Hungary and Poland lived essentially under the rule of the Kremlin for decades, and in those decades there was a cross-pollination of techniques and information that buoyed all of these athletes. We're talking about expertise handed down from coach to athlete, building up year after year. It's no wonder that Soviet bloc fencers rose to the top of the podium.

The Soviet Union officially dissolved the day after Christmas in 1991. On December 26th, the republics of the USSR were granted independence, ending decades of rule and intense rivalry. These newly independent countries have familiar names to us like the Ukraine and Russia. In practicality what this meant for fencers was a freedom from the totalitarian rule of the USSR and the ability to leave the country. They now could move out, could go to begin lives in other countries in whatever way they chose to. It also meant a loss of funding, which meant a much harder road for training in fencing. The choice to stay or go was a difficult one.

Not really amateurs

The Olympic Games and other major international tournaments like FIE Fencing World Cups are all touted as being for amateur athletes. What exactly is an amateur athlete? It's an athlete who does not get monetary compensation for their work in a sport. For a long time that included paid endorsements from companies as well as actual salary for doing the sport itself. This included famous American athlete Jim Thorpe, who was stripped of his medals in the 1912 Olympics after it was discovered that he accepted payment in sponsorship of during a couple of summers in college basketball. Amateur athletes were required by regulations to have other jobs besides working in sports. For example, instructors are not permitted to compete.

This has come to mean less in the last thirty years. Why? There are a couple of reasons. The first is that money talks, and it talked for the Olympics Bigger names brought bigger viewership and more money to the International Olympic Committee (IOC), so they relaxed their rules about sponsorship after the rise of television in the 1950's. The other reason is the Eastern bloc.

Athletes living and training in Soviet influenced countries were back door professional athletes from the outset. Their food, housing, training, and equipment were all paid for by the government. Exactly what a professional athlete in another country might get from a sponsor or through a salary for playing.

How did the USSR get around the requirement that athletes have jobs? Simple - Soviet athletes were given some position in the government or military which was what they were technically being compensated for rather than for their athletic training. It should be cleared up here that the Soviet Union was not the only country to do this in some form or fashion. Western countries like Italy, France, Germany, etc. are often granted positions in major government organizations like the police or military to afford them salaries to sustain them while they train without their having to resort to balancing work in the private sector. However, no one else did this practice anywhere close to the scale that the Soviet Union did, with government funded training facilities and coaches.

In the U.S., athletes had to hoof it to raise money to train through donations, family resources, and jobs unrelated to their sport in order to maintain their qualified status for the Olympics. That adds up to a great deal of time and stress that Soviet athletes simply didn't have to face. This system favored Soviet athletes inherently.

That is until the IOC recognized the problem and softened its stance through the 1970's and 1980's. The Dream Team, America's band of professional basketball players, stepped onto the court in the Olympic Games for the first time in Barcelona in 1992. With names like Charles Barkley and Magic Johnson, the team trounced its opponents while Michael Jordan spent late nights playing cards and days swinging his golf club rather than training or resting during his downtime while competing in the Olympics. It's notable that professional athletes aren't the only answer, as the United States basketball team fought bitterly to only a bronze in 2004.

For Soviet athletes, there was not the glory or massive cash flow that American professional athletes could attain, but these athletes also never had to sell homemade cookies or have a car wash to buy equipment. Soviet fencers could focus on their training instead of their living.

It's interesting to note that fencing is perhaps the only sport where the rule for professional athletes were bent from the very beginning. Fencing masters, who were technically professional, were part of the Olympics in the first two modern games in 1896 and 1900.

Military aspect

"The physical education of the rising generation is one of the necessary elements of the system of communist education of youth." Vladimir Lenin, 1920

The Soviet Union was by every measure a military state. The Red Army serviced the country in daily life in many ways. The military was incorporated into schools all the way down to young children, as well as into other aspects of community life. This extended heartily into sports, where the military sports programs permeated the Eastern bloc, searching for and fostering potential athletic champions from a young age. The best young athletes didn't just choose to come and train - the best were chosen by experts and groomed to win.

Coaches constantly scouted schools from the first grade forward, visiting PE classes in each school and grade to estimate the capabilities of each student. Then they invited the students that they deemed to have potential to come train in their sport section, which was of needless to say all free with all of the necessary equipment provided by the government. For working parents, this also provided a positive way for their children to be involved in something and to keep them from being idle. Many cities were not safe, and idle children could potentially get into trouble. So, because of these things, many children went on to do sports, and sports were promoted through all of society. It didn't hurt that these trainings were free through government sponsorship, and still are.

As mentioned before, dominance in the area of sport was seen as extension of dominance in culture and foreign policy. If the USSR could win in athletic competition, it meant that they were better than the United States. We can look at it much the same as we look at the space race, with countries trying to one up one another to get into space and then onto the moon first.

Translation: "We will start a Spartakiada of Soviet People with new victories in labor and in sports!"

All the way down the line, the Soviet Union created its sports infrastructure as an extension of it's military. Athletes had strict training regimens based on militaristic training principles. They got up early and their diets were monitored for maximum performance. Training extended all year, with experienced coaches pushing their athletes to their fullest potential. This required a great deal of discipline, but it also created powerful results that we can see on the podium in those years and even after. Even with kids, way before reaching international level, the kids were taken in the summer into these intense sport camps where they were trained hard from the morning to the evening, all summer long. Again, always free and provided by the government.

Under the USSR existed a system of training called the Unified Sports Classification System, established in 1935 (see Appendix D). It's a codified, quantified way to make sense of how athletes perform and what they need to do to improve. The scale goes from Third Class Junior Sportsman all the way to Merited Master of Sport (also called an Honored Master of Sport). The rating system was built on a series of competitions and adapted forms of this are still used today in many countries. A high sports ranking was looked up to with a huge amount of honor. If you reached the rank of Master of Sport in your sport, it was clear that you had made a significant achievement in the sport, but people all around the country outside of the sports world also paid a huge amount of respect to these individuals. Even small children knew what it meant to be a Master of Sport, whether they understood the sport in detail or not. This was true even for things that would be considered "niche" sports. All of this created a sense of social achievement and status within the community and the country, on a much bigger scale than anything in the rest of the world. This was then and is still now important in how children and then athletes train and approach the sport and competition in Russia.

This is just one example of how the USSR created a holistic and comprehensive training program to foster the best of the best in athletics.

Unlike the disjointed way that Western athletes train, which happens from the ground up, Soviet athletes came to their training from the top down. The structure was imposed through the government rather than being created by individuals. Though there were certainly a great deal of negative consequences for the Soviet people during the days of the USSR, it is undeniable that the methods they used effectively got them where they wanted to be. Gold medals.

That is something to meditate on. What cost is too high for athletic prowess? The goal of sport is to push the human body and mind as far as it can go, to raise us to our fullest potential.

Chapter 6: New talent in the USA

The world has always been a planet of immigrants. People move from here to there, migrating in search of a better life and better opportunities. That ebb and flow of human intellect and talent creates opportunities not just for the people who leave their homes for a new country, but also for the citizens of the country that they come to as those people now benefit from the expertise and creativity that these immigrants bring.

This is precisely what we see with fencing.

What happened in the Soviet Union in the late 80's and 90's created a domino effect that American fencers would feel much later. While the international relationships with the former Soviet bloc states remain contentious at best, the loss of the centralized government suddenly allowed the proven fencing practices used in the USSR to make their way across the ocean to America. Former foes were now able to benefit from the tactics that once eluded them.

Flood of fencing professionals

In the 1990's there was a flood of fencing professionals from the former Eastern bloc countries. Keep in mind that it wasn't just the USSR but many countries who saw a massive opening in the aftermath of the breakup of the Soviet Union. Professional fencers and coaches from Russia, Ukraine, Belarus, Poland, and other countries of the former Soviet Union and Warsaw bloc moved out of those places and to the United States with their families.

There are almost too many examples to name that came in this wave. One of the most prominent is Ed Korfanty, the number one saber coach in the USA and the man who groomed champions Mariel Zagunis, Rebecca Ward, and more to the top of the podium at the Olympics. Remember back to Chapter 4 and the revolution that saber fencing saw in the Olympics in the early 2000's. That massive change and the first wide wave of fencing medals can be directly attributed to the presence of Korfanty in the United States. Korfanty came to the United States from Poland in 1990 following a prolific career on the Polish National Team in the seventies and eighties.

Yury Gelman is also an example of a talented fencing coach who came to the United States in the 1990's following the breakup of the Soviet Union. Gelman trained fencers in Kiev from the late 1970's, serving as the coach for the Ukrainian Fencing Team from 1987-1991. His impact on fencing once he came to America is significant, having coached five American men's saber teams in the Olympics since 2000. His work with the Manhattan Fencing Club in the last nearly twenty years and the success he's bred there speak to the stellar knowledge that he brought with him from Kiev.

Another notable fencing coach from the USSR is Arkady Burdan. A two-time Olympic Fencing coach for the United States, Burdan was named USSR Master of Sports and Honored Coach of the Ukrainian Republic early in his career. Considered to be among the highest qualified fencing coaches in the world, he began teaching fencing in Atlanta in 1994 after an entire career as a powerhouse fencing coach for the Ukrainian Olympic Training Center.

Simon Gershon, coach of the 1986 Gold Medal World Champion Russian Women's Foil Team, went on to coach Olympians Miles Chamley-Watson and Nicole Ross for the United States in the 2012 Games and numerous other American athletes in international competitions. He's now based at the Fencer's Club in New York City.

The head coach of fencing at Penn State, Emmanuil Kaidanov is the all-time most successful NCAA coach in fencing history. He has coached ten Olympians and stands with a total record of 832-89 over three decades of coaching on the collegiate level. He came to the United States all the way back in 1979 from the Soviet Union, bringing with him fencing and coaching prowess that would go on to dominate the sport from the university level.

Andrey Geva came to Houston from the Soviet Union after making it to the highest echelons of fencing in his home country, only to miss his last national team by one touch. He brought fencing to Texas, founding the Alliance Fencing Academy and building his reputation among epee fencers to the point of becoming the designated coach for the women's epee team for the United States, leading them in the Rio Olympics and a World Champion title in 2018.

Epee fencer Gago Demirchian was born in Armenia and went on to fence in the USSR National championship after becoming a three-time Armenian National Champion. His father, Eduoard Demirchian, coached the Armenian National Epee team, and Gago certainly followed in his footsteps when he immigrated to the United States to become and epee coach. The younger Demirchian has been a U.S. national epee coach, with many of his Los Angeles based students becoming national champions, world champions, and Olympians.

Ukrainian Misha Itkin is also now based out of Los Angeles. He was a U.S. National foil coach for seven years and has coached a whole host of national and international competitors, including his son Nikita Itkin, the 2018 Individual Foil Men's Junior World Champion and a member of 2019 Senior Men's Foil Team. The elder Itkin is a foil champion himself before immigrating to the United States.

Aladar Kogler, a member of the USA Fencing Hall of Fame, was born in Hungary but spent nearly two decades at Columbia University, where he coached his fencers to a remarkable 449-123 record. Prior to coming to the United States, Kogler coached the Czechoslovakian National Fencing Team, where he led his fencers to success at the world championships and the Olympics. Kogler coached twenty U.S. Olympians over five Olympic Games. He's the author of ten books and twenty-five scientific papers surrounding the sport, relying on both his doctoral academic credentials and on his vast experience as a coach and fencer. Kogler stands as one of the most prominent names in U.S. Fencing.

These are only a few examples of the most highly accomplished fencing coaches to come out of the Soviet bloc following the fall of the USSR. If you were to walk into a large fencing club almost anywhere in the United States, you would find a legacy of training from immigrants who brought their fencing knowledge with them from these countries. While there are no hard numbers as to exactly how many fencing champions and coaches came to America in the 1990's and on to today, it's nonetheless a reality on the ground for competitive fencers that these coaches are here and supporting their progress.

Eastern bloc philosophy

We cannot go on here without talking about the grit and determination of the people of the Eastern bloc. It's one thing to look at how the government shaped these athletes in a broad sense through systematized training, but it's another that their skill and talent translated to success outside of that structure.

One of the hugely positive qualities that these fencing professionals bring with them is the deep sense of community. No one is in this alone, no fencer and no fencing family. You can see that in the fencing clubs that they run and in the close bonds that coaches form with their fencing students. While that drive to win is deeply embedded in the philosophy of Warsaw bloc coaches, it does not overshadow the belief that the real value comes in the personal growth that fencers experience through training and competition.

Grit and determination are another facet to the philosophy of the fencing coaches who came to the United States in the aftermath of the fall of the Soviet Union. Native born citizens often don't comprehend what a giant leap it is to move to the other side of the world and start over. It requires grit. It requires sacrifice. It requires self-belief and determination. Coaches who came here from the Eastern bloc brought that with them to their fencing clubs. The rigid rules and regulations which governed the sport training system in the USSR mandated grit and determination in order to rise to the top, and these coaches who came to the United States were at the top in their home countries.

Ambition is an integral part of the equation if one wants to get to the top of the world in anything. The fencing professionals who came from the former Eastern bloc countries had been part of a huge machine that thrust them forward towards greatness. These people brought that thirst for greatness with them when they came to the United States. No shortcuts, no quick road to success, no getting around the hard work that it takes to make it. The rigid structures from the state sponsored training programs were adapted on American shores and utilized to achieve the success that they hungered for. What's more, they instilled those same ethics into their fencing students.

International nature of sport in USA

America is a melting pot. With the exception of a very small minority of Native Americans, everyone who is here is descended from an immigrant. The international nature of life has translated into an international nature in the sport culture of the United States.

Athletics in the U.S. are anything but homogenous. Fencing is no different, and maybe even more international than other more mainstream sports.

When you walk into a fencing club, you'll generally find people from a great variety of backgrounds and ethnicities. It's one of the most beautiful parts of our sport! Fencers from all over the world train together and compete together under one flag, the flag of the United States. When these former Soviet fencing coaches came to the United States, they were able to integrate into the sport culture of America. It's through this integration that they built a network of success for their students. It's through this integration they were able to create a fencing training strategy unfettered by the constraints that they previously worked under.

This is not a new thing in America. Athletes have been coming here to train and compete for the Olympics and other international competitions for over a hundred years. For whatever problems here are here, people continue to come to pursue their dreams with likeminded colleagues and to raise the bar for performance in sport. It's good for everyone, and we consistently see the fruit of that teamwork on the international stage for fencing.

Chapter 7: Niche Nature

There are multiple factors at play in the rise of American fencing, far more than the influx of talented coaches due to geopolitical changes. Other factors include how American sport culture and specifically the size of the fencing community create a positive incubator for talent.

In the wider context of sport in America, fencing holds a distinction as being a very niche sport. The community is relatively small, the equipment specialized, and the opportunities to train scattered across the country. The word "niche" implies a high level of adaptability to the environment, as when animals adapt to master a specific sector of their environment. The notion of mastery is inherent here!

Though pretty much everyone knows that fencing is sport sword fighting, few Americans know the ins and outs of the sport in any kind of detailed way. In the United States it is closely associated with the Olympic Games in much the same way that sports like curling or bobsledding are, meaning that most Americans only think about fencing once every four years.

The size of fencing in across the world isn't huge either. Even the countries who have long dominate the sport like Hungary and Russia still have a low level of participation compared to other more mainstream sports like soccer or hockey.

How big is fencing?

In the United States there are roughly seven hundred fencing clubs currently registered with the USA Fencing. That sounds like a lot at first blush, but consider that there might be, say ten or twenty martial arts dojos in any medium sized city compared with perhaps five fencing clubs in a whole state and you quickly see how small the sport truly is.

A quick search of "martial arts near me" came up with more than five hundred studios, all within an hour or two drive of my home. Compare that to fencing schools, of which there are five within an hour drive of where I live. There are more martial arts schools within any given metropolitan area than there are fencing schools in the entire United States! It's just a mind-blowing idea.

Let's keep going with that comparison. USA Fencing (or as sometimes called USFA), the governing body of fencing in America, has about 30,000 members across the United States. In contrast to that level of membership, here are membership numbers on other governing organizations.

- US Quidditch - 4,000 members, 200 teams
- USA Table Tennis - 9,000 members
- US Rowing - 14,000 individual members, 1,050 organizational members
- United States Chess Federation - 85,000 members
- USA Track and Field - 130,000 members
- USA Wrestling - 159,000 members, 2,900 clubs
- US Figure Skating - 178,000 members
- USA Gymnastics - 200,000 members
- USA Swimming - 400,000 members
- USA Softball - 1.3 million players, 300,000 coaches
- US Youth Soccer - 3 million players from age 4-19

Within the confines of American sports, it could be argued that fencing is a niche inside a niche. It is important to note that, while fencing is dwarfed by many larger sports in the United States, it's still far from the smallest. There are plenty of tiny sports, many of them Olympic sports that have fewer participants than fencing. However, in the scope of major sports worldwide, fencing is nowhere close.

It's notable that this is not the case everywhere. France and Italy for example have a much higher profile for fencing. While it doesn't come close to the popularity of other sports within these countries, the long history of fencing does still lend a weight of seriousness to the sport. There is a respect for the sport of fencing, almost a nobility to it in these places that translates to widespread recognition in a way that has happened little in the United States thus far.

Niche sporting in context

There are two ways to view the niche nature of fencing. Either it's a negative trait that holds the sport back OR it's a positive trait that fosters a close community.

It's absolutely the latter.

Fencing in the United States and in fact across the globe doesn't need to be massive in order to foster highly capable athletes who improve the sport. In fact, the lack of popularity can perhaps buoy fencing towards a bolder vision that's executed without the interference of a wide public that is not as invested in the sport. That's not to say that it's not a great thing that every other child plays soccer, but it is to say that it's not necessary for a sport to be in every little town in order to be valuable. Bigger does not mean better.

What is true is that fencing has enough prominence to be an Olympic sport, which gives it a level of recognition and interest to fuel interest and membership. Moreover, fencing been in every Olympic Games since their establishment. There are some fencing celebrities that are well-known within the world of fencing, Bach, Kolobkov, Vezzali, Flessel-Colovic, etc. Even in the United States, where fencing is less popular than it is in Europe and even in some parts of Asia, world class fencers are increasingly being recognized in the media.

Social media and online streaming contribute to this fanning out of support. The numbers are still tiny for fencing on social media compared to even less well-known members of other sports like baseball or soccer.

The fencer with the most Instagram followers as of this writing is by far Ibtihaj Muhammad with right at three hundred thousand, all other top fencers are well below one hundred thousand. Compare that to soccer player Leo Messi with over a hundred and ten million followers or gymnast Simone Biles with three and a half million followers, and it's plain to see that fencing isn't close to being there yet.

A balancing act

One thing that more support equates to is a firmer financial foundation for fencers. Fencers are increasingly visible in the United States, with names like Race Imboden and Ibtihaj Muhammad pushing further into the mainstream media world. However, these fencers aren't famous just for their fencing, they've launched into the spotlight for other reasons.

Ibtihaj is well known for being the first woman in hijab to compete in the Olympics and medal, but then she leveraged that spark of press to support her work with minority issues, building girl's self-esteem, and naturally highlighting fencing. Race is widely known because he is a now a model, which is not directly related to fencing except that he was scouted at the Olympic Games while fencing. Most fencers don't have that kind of media exposure that's why it is very difficult to sustain on a senior level.

- Higher media exposure means better endorsements.
- Better endorsements mean more money.
- More money means more focused training.
- More focused training means higher performance on the international stage.
- Higher performance on the international stage means higher media exposure.
- Higher media exposure means better endorsements.

This is the chicken and the egg game that niche sports like fencing fall into. It's a balancing act that every fencer finds themselves in once they get to a certain level. When more fencers are in the media, it attracts more young people to fencing. This sport has been steadily growing over the last twenty years, with new fencing clubs opening up and established fencing clubs expanding to accommodate this growth.

It is unlikely that fencing will ever cross over into anything beyond a niche sport. For one thing, it's not a team sport. Individual sports have a tough time making it to the top of the heap. Of the top ten sports globally, three are individual including golf, tennis, and table tennis. Team sports tend to become much higher profile than individual sports. Part of that might have to do with the lower participation of individual sports, along with the higher cost of lessons and training.

That still leaves fencing plenty of room to grow within its niche and to adapt effectively. Remember that the definition of a niche sport includes the caveat that it includes mastery within that small area that it occupies. It's being part of something special. While there might be three million kids playing soccer in the United States, fencers get the benefit of being a part of something unique.

The benefits of community

A major reason that fencing in America is becoming so successful is the community that surrounds the sport. Fencing is a small enough community to truly be a community. Fencers and coaches who compete on the national circuit get to know one another over the course of their competitive time.

For example, let's do some simple math. Of course this math isn't perfectly exact, but it's good enough to give us an accurate picture.

- There are about 18,000 fencers of school age in fencing (born 2001-2012).
- Given there are 2 genders and 3 weapons, and assuming, for the sake of discussion as we know this isn't exactly true, that each gender/weapon/age have similar number of fencers, we get: 2*3*12=72 categories (age/weapon/gender)
- That gives us 236 people in each category - in the entire country!

But if we go deeper and get more specific, using just a couple of birth years as an example,

- 2001 - 1,510 (Men - 976, Women - 535), out of which only 1,123 are competitive
- 2002 - 1,889 (Men - 1229, Women - 661), out of which only 1,337 are competitive

So that means that there are about 200 people competing in a specific category at all. And of course, at the competitive level that's a bit higher, say we call it a highly competitive level if a fencer got rating, the numbers drop significantly:

- For 2002 there are about:
    - 180 rated sabreists (M - 118, W - 62)
    - 276 rated epeeists (M - 156, W - 90)
    - 235 rated foilists (M - 153, W - 82)

What does this mean? This mean that after competing for a while in your own age category on a national level you would know EVERYONE! Less than one hundred competitors, that you see over and over again at competitions over the course of years. Keep in mind, this isn't just one season, this happens year after year. At competitions, there's a great deal of down time. You're only up there fencing for a few minutes at a time, and then you've got hours of waiting. Once a fencer is eliminated or is waiting for their next round, they get to sit and watch other matches, often with rival fencers who are waiting or have been eliminated. Sure they go and focus too, or brush up with their coaches, or rest, but they also hang out. That connection is important, and it fosters lifelong relationships with fencers in their age range.

Some of the benefits that the community aspect of fencing brings to the young athletes that it fosters are:

- Positive and supportive peer relationships
- Positive and supportive mentor relationships
- Decision making opportunities
- Tailored experiences to individual needs
- Camaraderie with individual across diverse backgrounds
- Sense of holding a meaningful place within the sporting community
- Ability to network with other fencers across levels

There is an accessibility within the fencing community that helps to grow great fencers compared to larger sports. The odds of meeting or training with a top football player or football coach for an aspiring NFL player are miniscule at best. For fencers, the size of the sport and the tight knit nature of the community means that those coaches and Olympians are within reach for fencers who put in time and effort. Actually in almost any given national tournament (North America Cup, July Challenge, of Division 1 Championships) USA national team members, including Olympic and World Champions and Medalists will participate on equal grounds with everybody else.

Inspiration is a critical component of aspiration. Without the tight community that fencing in America offers, it's doubtful that the level of fencing coming out of the States would be as high. The niche sport community of fencing gives fencers a solid, fertile background to build from towards greatness.

Chapter 8: Fencing Across the USA

The structure of fencing training in the United States is a major contributor to the ability of American fencers to rise in prominence. What's been developed in the United States is totally different than what happens in other parts of the world, though the fascinating part is how American fencing has molded to fill what are seemingly universal needs in the sport. The mechanisms through which those needs are filled are unique to the United States!

Where the fencing schools of Europe are rooted in centuries-old entrenched techniques and the Eastern bloc fencing schools are rooted in a top-down government supported structure from the 20th century, fencing schools in the United States are community driven ventures born of entrepreneurial spirit. Fencing clubs have risen across the USA, from coast to coast, as both European immigrants and homegrown fencing champions have settled in areas of the country that felt like home to them. Each individual club is unique in its character, bolstered by regional norms and local flavor.

The fencing clubs in Houston are distinct from the fencing clubs of Chicago. Increasingly in American fencing, we're seeing that having a large pool of fencers who bring a variety of perspectives to the sport allows fencing to grow richer with each generation. Rather than being a homogeneous system, there is a tapestry of experiences woven together.

Just as the United States itself is stronger for being a melting pot of cultures and individuals, so too is American fencing stronger for being a melting pot of styles and backgrounds. Through diversity there is strength.

Mindset of American fencing

The oldest fencing club in America, The Fencers Club in New York City, opened in 1883. Its mission for more than a century has been to promote excellence through fencing, intertwining public service and personal growth with sport fencing. What makes this club a model of American fencing is that community and growth mindset.

Many fencing clubs in the United States offer access to fencing for individuals who would generally be able to afford fencing, including The Fencers Club. It's a central part of the mindset of American fencing. The most prominent non-profit program is run by Peter Westbrook, and it is a fantastic example that this is not a sport for the social elite only. The reason is that fencing in America is fundamentally not a sport for the socially elite as it traditionally was in Europe and elsewhere. There is a strong sense of egalitarianism in the U.S. fencing community. There is an abiding sense among members of the American fencing community that this sport has the ability to open doors and to facilitate self-improvement.

This notion of equality translates into success, as fencers in the United States rise in the sport through personal passion rather than through a societally imposed structure. With the incredible variety of choice available for sports enthusiasts in the United States, fencers tend to choose this sport and stick with it because they are passionate about it. Autonomy can equal powerful enthusiasm, which translates to the success we've seen.

Fencing in the United States is a sport that promotes equality. Race, gender, social standing, religion, culture, etc. all fall away on the strip. We can see this exemplified all the way to the top echelon of fencers. Peter Westbrook, the African-American sabre fencer who brought home the first fencing medal for the United States in decades. Ibtihaj Muhammad, the first American Olympian to compete wearing a hijab. I believe the true nature of the sport promotes equality to start with. Because in fencing you can be a boy or a girl, short or tall, thick or thin, and still have an equal amount of success. Moreover, this sport does not rely on physical strength and often there are local competitions that are co-ed. In addition, having a uniform that covers the whole body gives the ability for every religion to compete without hindrance.

In the United States, this sport fosters athletes from all nationalities and backgrounds. It's key to the success of American fencers. As the sport has become increasingly integrated since the latter half of the last century, we have seen a rise in the American prowess in fencing. The bottom line here is that the more open a sport is to athletes of all backgrounds, the better its athletes will be. As American fencing has opened up to not only allow these diverse athletes but to in fact seek them out, the ability of these fencers to win internationally has risen.

Women fencers have particularly benefited from improved openness in the sport. Take the dominance of American female saber fencers from their integration into the Olympics at the turn of the millennium. As soon as women's saber began on the Olympic level, American women saber fencers were right there at the top of the podium. This has everything to do with the mindset of equality in American fencing schools, which across the board support increased inclusion of girls and women in fencing.

In fact, there is generally a push towards gender equity in fencing schools in America as a tool of empowerment and self-esteem building. There is still considerable inequity between the number of male fencers and the number of female fencers in the United States however, with roughly one third the number of women and girls earning USFA rankings in the sport. Women have lagged behind men in fencing participation across the world, due almost entirely to restrictions that kept them from participating in the sport. As those restrictions on competition have lifted and attitudes have changed, women have been drawn to competitive fencing.

When you look at the increased successes of American fencers on the international stage, it's clear that diversity is a driving factor. That diversity didn't just happen, it's a representation of the mindset of American fencing. And it works.

Club structure in the United States

Fencing clubs in America are borne of the entrepreneurial spirit that is intrinsic in our culture. Clubs in the United States rise up from an individual or a small group of individuals who love the sport and so jump in to form an organization. We consistently see fencing clubs that embrace the small business model, oftentimes run by families or coaches who put their life's work into the fencing club. Fencing schools in America often become like family themselves, with close community ties and supportive environments for members. It's a model that's increasingly popular, forging close relationships for team members as they navigate the sport.

Sanctioning of fencing clubs in the U.S. comes from the USA Fencing (often called by its previous name USFA, which stands for United States Fencing Association), a non-profit governing body which regulates sport of fencing and competition across the country in accordance with a strict set of rules and regulations and in association with the Fédération Internationale d'Escrime (FIE), the international governing body of the sport of fencing.

What's wonderful about the fencing club structure in the United States is the competitive and communal balance. Clubs are encouraged to innovate in teaching techniques in order to gain an edge on rival clubs through the free market. Rivalry and competition are real, and they push the sport forward - after all fencing clubs are vying for the fencers and the titles that will attract new members. Still, the fencing community, even between rival clubs, is on the whole respectful and encouraging.

Variety in outlook

One of the most surprising and fun things about fencing in America is that it's all different!

There are plenty of tiny fencing classes that are held outside of fencing clubs in smaller cities and rural areas across the country, fueling the love of fencing. Dance studios, community centers, martial arts schools, college or school sport courts, and more have become places for people to don fencing gear and practice swordsmanship.

These classes might not be a direct line to high level fencing competitions and international glory for American fencers, but they do stoke the fire for fencing as a sport and raise awareness.

Those are important roles in and of themselves. We cannot discount the value of a love of the sport, because as much as the Olympic Games and international competitions matter, they are not the real reason behind the pursuit of fencing. American fencing is grounded in a love of personal growth and the joy of pushing ourselves to be more than what we are. That's the driving passion behind every successful fencing club in the United States. Keep in mind that every single one of the big fencing clubs today started our very small and then developed. It has taken decades for the great fencing schools of the United States to find their feet! We must allow and encourage smaller fencing venues to continue to train for the love of the sport.

What we must remember is that the fencing club structure in America is it's something all its own. It's continuing to grow and evolve. That growth and evolution is obviously going in the right direction, but as it turns out, the fencing club structure is only one piece of the puzzle.

Chapter 9: The Power of University Training

The university training system in American fencing has proven to be a powerhouse for American fencers, dramatically shaping the path of training for those who compete on the world stage under the stars and stripes. This network of elite colleges is completely unlike anything that can be found anywhere else in the world, but it serves to fulfill the same purpose as many of the other structures that countries have in place to train their fencers.

The university system in fencing provides an infrastructure for training for four years that allows fencers to pursue their fencing career nationally and internationally without jeopardizing their work. There are still the demands of college coursework yes, but those demands are not the same as the demands of a career. What other countries provide through the government, the USA enables through the university sport system.

Professional athletes willing to achieve international results must have several hours a day of practice, must have an immediate access to training facilities, to medical personnel, etc. The university gives all of these things, including great coaches, access to all above, support for high level competitions like the NAC with travel and registration expenses paid for. Not only that, but there is the fantastic competitive experience within the NCAA, which is not only open to Americans. Often fencing on the NCAA circuit gives a great opportunity competitively for fencers to challenge themselves against the international competition. This is truly a unique opportunity for fencers to compete on that international level without having to concentrate on their future or how to provide for themselves. It's all focused - train, compete, study, repeat. Oftentimes these top NCAA athletes are actually members of the national team. That's a great arrangement and a great opportunity to continue that fencing career before the real world of work and finances hit them.

The point is this - the requirements for top contenders to compete are universal. They are the same for all countries. What changes is how a given country ends up making that happen. America has always been this great experiment, a place to try new ways of living and see if the individual can succeed. In this instance, Americans have blazed a unique trail for its fencers, and as it turns out the university system is a perfect fit for this purpose.

University structure in the United States

There is not only a powerful club structure in the United States, there is also a potent university structure for fencing. Governed by a combination of the National Collegiate Athletic Association (NCAA) and the USA Fencing, the NCAA Fencing Championships offer American fencers another avenue to grow and create success in the sport.

Nearly fifty colleges and universities in the U.S. have fencing teams that participate in the NCAA. Each of these school teams offers fencers an additional route to training and support, often with scholarship opportunities for fencers. This is essentially another layer of training for fencers in the U.S. that has been a boost for fencers across the country. Top level, Ivy League and ACC University fencing teams are a force in domestic fencing.

Many members of the U.S. Olympic Fencing team, including a hefty number of medalists from the last two decades, are products of NCAA fencing programs. Here are just a few:

- Gerek Meinhardt, the first male fencer from the United States to win a medal at the Senior World Championship in 2010 and the first American man to reach #1 FIE ranking, fenced for the University of Notre Dame.
- Lee Kiefer, the youngest American fencer to medal at the World Championship in 2011, and one of the top-level world fencers, fenced for Notre Dame, winning NCAA title 4 times in the row.
- Rio Olympic silver medalist Alexander Massialas fenced for Stanford.
- Nzingha Prescod, women's foilist on the 2016 US Olympic team, won the Ivy League Rookie of the Year award while attending Columbia University
- Olympic foilist Miles Chamley-Watson won 2 NCAA Championships while fencing for Penn State.
- Mariel Zagunis is a four-time Olympic sabre fencer with gold in 2004 and 2008, she won her

seventh World Champion title while attending the University of Notre Dame
- Eli Dershwitz is the #1 sabre fencer in the world as of July 2018, fences for the Harvard Crimson
- The list goes on and on...

These fencers didn't start fencing when they went to university but came up through clubs across the country before refining their skills on their college fencing teams. Coaches come through the structure of university fencing programs, with many of our top support members for U.S. fencers either coaching or competing at the collegiate level.

A notable aspect of university fencing in America is that top level academic universities go hand in hand with top level fencing schools. Ivy League universities like Princeton, Yale, Columbia, and Harvard, as well as top ten schools like Stanford and Duke also have highly ranked fencing programs. The stature of the universities themselves has gone a long way towards attracting top coaches and students. Note that fencers who attend these universities must also gain acceptance to the schools, meaning they have to hold their own academically. It's not uncommon for fencers to start in the sport because they love it, then later find that it's a fantastic opportunity to support their college goals and also continue their sport career.

It's notable here that university students at private, non-profit, high level schools often end up paying less out of pocket than lower tiered states schools thanks to the abundance of grant and scholarship money available to them. Fencers who make it to a Division I NCAA school find themselves well positioned to take advantage of a wide variety of supports, both financial and otherwise.

The university system in the United States is a major reason that fencing has grown into the prestige sport that it is, associated with intellect and excellence.

University fencing = Soviet bloc training

When young person goes to university and becomes a member of that school's fencing team, their situation is remarkably similar to what you find in Soviet bloc training.

For four years, fencers have the luxury of not having to pursue a career and fence simultaneously. Naturally they still have their university studies to consider, but as anyone who has made the transition from college to the real world will tell you, the pressures are not the same. We cannot overstate how much split attention affects the ability of an athlete to perform well. This is a major reason that Soviet bloc athletes were able to run rampant on the international stage, they could put their focus on their athleticism.

The financial support of the university system is another major focus factor that equates to the Soviet bloc athletes. Universities often pick up the tab for competitions, just as their Cold War counterparts did. Those fees add up quickly, easily to thousands of dollars per year. Not only are the fees picked up but travel to competitions as well. All of that means fencers spending less time worrying about dollars and more time worrying about defeating an opponent. Though fencers who make it to the Olympic level can spin their success into endorsements that allow them time and focus to train, getting to that level is tough without the support of something like the university system.

The structure of college fencing is not unlike the structure of Eastern training. In fact, Russian athletes attended, and still do attend, boarding schools specifically designed to give them the right training to become elite competitors. Just as in those schools, U.S. university athletes live close to their facility, they have access to facilities both for fencing and for cross training, food is right there and easy to get to, and they are constantly surrounded with reinforcements to propel them forward. That communal aspect is important, and it works. Unfractured, focused training is key.

Universities have another big thing going for them - coaches. School sports programs have deep pockets, and so they can afford to lure great fencing coaches to train their athletes. Of course, this is very much the same as in the Eastern bloc. It's not just the money that's alluring, it's also the stability. Colleges can give perks and benefits to coaches, things like healthcare, facilities, and childcare. That can be a powerful draw for a fencing coach as opposed to the muscle of running their own fencing club. Coaches on the university level, like Vladimir Nazlymov of the Ohio State University and Andy Ma of Penn State build programs over the course of many years that support fencers through to the internationally competitive level.

Chapter 10: System of Competitions

While no one thing is the reason for American fencing's meteoric rise over the course of the past 20 years, the system of competitions in the United States is undoubtedly the deciding factor. No level of coaching influx, club support, or even indomitable American spirit could have gotten us here without a structure that fostered competition. The fencing tournament system in the United States has improved tremendously in the last several decades, becoming refined to the point that it is now made for creating international competitors.

Getting started young

Starting from the age as early as seven and even six, fencers in the United States have the opportunity to compete at the local level and to progress through the USFA competition system to the regional and national level. Starting young is a major factor for fencers, in part because it plays into the long game of the sport. Internationally competitive fencers can participate in the sport well into their thirties and beyond, all the way through elite competitions like the Olympics.

High level competition extends to the highly developed system of veteran fencing, which is well developed in the United States from the local to the regional to the national level. That means that a fencer who begins competing on the national level in the United States at the age of seven has decades worth of time to compete, potentially more than twenty or even thirty years on the senior level alone.

It's impossible to overstate the importance of longevity in the sport. In fencing, unlike many other sports, you can reach a success no matter when you started. There are examples of USA Olympians that started well in their middle school and succeeded on the International level, but there are also many examples of fencers who started later or earlier. The sport is continuing to skew younger with each passing year as parents discover it and sign their kids up earlier. These kids start competing early and so develop the skill of turning on their competitive brain and turning off their training brain when the time comes. They learn to train more effectively and to flow with the rhythm of the competitive fencing season.

The human brain is more malleable and elastic at a younger age than it is for adults. This is true in everything from learning new languages to riding a bike. Old habits and ways of thinking die hard. Those habits carry on through a competitive fencing career, which can last well into an individual's thirties without blinking. Competitive fencers, barring any complicated health issues, can expect to enjoy competing even at the international level into their fifties and sixties.

Fencing is increasingly part of the youth sports culture in the United States. During those late elementary, middle, and high school years, fencing clubs in America have open classes for kids to start in the sport just is the case for ubiquitous childhood activities like soccer or dance. That focus on extracurricular activities as essential pieces of youth development has been beneficial for fencing as a sport on the international stage. American parents want to raise well rounded children, and fencing holds a growing stature as a way to foster that.

Parents really are the drivers of their kids' future in the USA. There's the cliché "Behind every successful athlete is her mom", and it's a cliché for a reason. It's true. The parents who are the most ambitious have the kids who are the most ambitious. This goes for kids that work hard to reach their goal and thus most of them will have opportunities to travel and learn. A major mark of the structure of fencing in America is that there is no "quota" for how many competitions, local or non-local, that a child has to go to per the coach or per some centralized budget as is the way in other countries, i.e. Russia or the old Soviet bloc. Parents in America can provide as many opportunities to the kids as they can support financially. That's just fantastic for fencers and fencing in general, even though it can weight things to one side.

U.S. Fencing's competitive hierarchy

The first thing to know and that we have mentioned previously is that fencing in America is governed by the USFA, the United States Fencing Association, which is nowadays called USA Fencing. This non-profit governing body sets forward the rules and regulations for sport fencing in the United States for fencing clubs to follow. Additionally and importantly, the USFA structures the competition circuit. It works closely with FIE, the international governing body of fencing in adapting the rules and following the international competitive calendar. The Olympic organization is completely separate.

Every sport has its peculiarities and unique competition structure. To explain the fencing competitive structure, it's beneficial to start at the top and work down. Fencing competitions in the U.S. are broken down into four major types:

- National
- Regional
- Divisional
- Local

Local competitions are generally out of the hierarchical structure as they do not directly feed into other forms of competition. They are a marvelous and accessible method for grooming young fencers for an edge in competition. Accessibility is the key word here, as they allow fencers to try out competitive fencing with little commitment and less pressure. Local competitions are the central gateway that foster the growth of competitive fencers who then rise up.

Regional and divisional competitions feed into the national competitions. The basic structure of U.S. fencing tournaments has remained the same for decades in terms of raising fencers for qualification on the national and eventually international level. The particulars within the structure do get updated periodically. There is a stalwart sense to the American competitive fencing structure, and fencers have grown to trust that structure as they train and move forward. That kind of stability is important for fostering generational fencing knowledge in the United States, a point we've mentioned before.

Regional tournaments offer fencers the chance to compete in mid-level competition between the local and national levels. This is by far the biggest competitive circuit in American fencing, and it's where fencers learn how to compete well. In many ways this is the training ground of our fencing champions. The regional nature of these tournaments means that fencers learn how to navigate performing while they travel, a massively important skill for fencers to have if they are to compete in larger venues. Because they are in the general area of the city that a fencer lives, they aren't as expensive to get to or as difficult to travel to as national competitions. It's a tiered way to support and grow talented fencers from the ground up.

Divisionals offer fencers the opportunity to fence on a high level while also potentially leading them to national championships. Most divisional competitions are last minute qualifiers for national championships. It's the one-time nature of these competitions that makes them something truly extraordinary, because fencers at this level are then able to get into a national level competition without having to chase points across a season. That increases the pressure and the need for that "competition brain". With only the top one quarter of fencers making it to the next level, the stakes are high in divisionals in a way that's similar to international competition.

National level fencing competitions challenge fencers to become the best they possibly can be. These fencing tournaments bring together athletes from across the country, offering them the opportunity to see what fencers everywhere in the United States are doing in terms of technique, training, and style. This level of competition is palpably different than anything else you'll find in tournaments in the United States, and they give fencers the closest thing to a taste of international competition. For the most part, national level competitions are only available to fencers who qualify through competing in other competitions. The tiered structure mimics the qualification paths for international competitions, essentially grooming American fencers for the worldwide platforms.

Outside of strictly domestic competitions in the United States like Fencing Summer Nationals and the July Challenge are the Junior Olympics. The Junior Olympics are connected to international competitions – the Junior and Cadet World Championship, Division 1 Championships are connected to Senior World Fencing Championship and Veteran age championships are connected to Veteran World Fencing Championships. That means that each of these championships serve as a last qualifying event to earn points and get to the respective world team.

Special features of the American system

There are several very particular facets to the American system that are unique, that make it work so well.

First off, cross age competition is a regular theme. This pushes everyone up. Thirteen-year-olds for example can potentially participate in as many as six age groups - Y14, Cadet, Junior, and Seniors Division 1A, Seniors Division 2 and Seniors Division 3 or Division 1 (based on either C and higher or D and lower). Not just individually though. They can also participate on all the respective teams related to these, so the Y14 Team, Cadet Team, Junior Team, and Senior Team. This is a lot of ways to fence and many of this age do it! This pushes them forward in a big way, elevating them to compete against fencers who are much more rigorous than they would be able to fence against if they were only in divisions with their own age.

Another major boon for American fencers are the fencing marathons that are regularly part of the competitive circuit. These are unlike anything elsewhere, and they develop a fencing stamina which is quite unprecedented. In the example above of a thirteen-year-old fencer, that fencer from a very young age competes for several days non-stop in very high-level competitions. Here's another example. At U.S. Fencing Summer Nationals, a C-rated fourteen-year-old fencer can compete in seven or even eight events in the course of ten days. In this case that would be Y14, Cadet, Junior, Division 1A, Division 1, Division 2 and Division 3, and the Senior team. Division 3 would be if he or she qualified to Division 3 before upgrading their rating to C and also qualifying for Division 1. This definitely requires a lot of stamina, both physical and mental. With that kind of focus and follow through, fencers who compete like this get a leg up on competitors.

Even the structure of the competition circuit "forces" fencers to seek qualification to nationals, and thus pushes them forward. There are constant carrots for fencers to push their rating higher, to qualify in further events, and to compete more regularly in order to get to that next level. Supporting the national events are regional events, which provide a fantastic opportunity to grow quickly beyond the confines of one single geographical area but without going too terribly far from home. This is an excellent model for fencers to start to experience from a young age.

Speaking of travel, for fencers in the United States this is a regular thing. Granted, it requires quite a hefty financial commitment on parents and families, but if we ignore this aspect and focus on pure fencing benefits, this is an absolutely great thing. It allows American kids to be exposed to huge variety of fencing. They are able to become accustomed to fencing in new venues with unknown opponents. In sport, as in so many things, practice makes perfect. Fencers are able to practice competing in new environments, and this makes the transition to fencing in the international circuits much easier. Now you might be flying across an ocean instead of across the country, but you are still flying and have learned how to pack your gear and manage yourself in unfamiliar places while still fencing you best.

Quickly navigating to the national level is not only essential, but it's also laid out beautifully for fencers. It's possible to move very quickly to the national level and qualify for Fencing Summer Nationals. This is where fencers can jump in and compete against the best in the country. Though it happens quickly, these fencers learn and grow quickly. National level exposure adds an oil to the fire, always. With the huge success of Zagunis, Massialas, Homer, Imboden, Chamley-Watson, Dershwitz and Muhammad, fencers are suddenly able to reach their heroes. It's a major incentive, and major motivator for young fencers.

Up until the national championships, all USA competitions are open to non-citizens. This means that all fencers from any country can participate in everything. We often see at NACs and all regional tournaments fencers from Canada, Mexico, Puerto Rico, China and other countries. Even at youth level. This creates even more "international" level competition here locally. There is a rich web of fencers from all over the world who travel to participate in competitions here in the United States, such is the quality of the competitive tournament structure here.

And again, we must relay the importance of the university structure. In the United States it is also closely tied to the ambitions of parents. Towards the cadet and junior ages, parents of those competitive fencers and indeed the fencers themselves are aware of the huge benefits of fencing in college. Of course, they start fencing because they love it and have passion, but once they discover it's also a huge college bound benefit, why not go for it in college? Leaning towards the college entrance, many fencers start putting in the extra effort, and that's a double win, since it pushes not only themselves, but others. The club, the town, and every competition they go to rise to the level of competition. This then spins into the university fencing system, so that the competition and the university system are synergistic in this way.

Willingness to adapt

The basic structure of fencing competition in the United States has not changed in decades, but there is constant tweaking and adaptation to improve the sport.

A great example of this is the addition of the Super Youth Circuit (SYC) as a means to qualification for Fencing Summer Nationals, allowing Y10 and Y12 fencers an additional path to the biggest competition in the United States while also establishing another valuable competitive experience for these fencers. The SYC circuit was so successful in fact that a Super Junior Cadet Circuit (SJCC) was introduced in 2018-2019 season and was a great success, to be continued in the following seasons. These additional competitions give American fencers critical levels of experience that prepares them more effectively for next level fencing.

Another recent example is the addition of the International Regional Circuit as a qualifying pathway to Fencing Summer Nationals for American fencers living abroad. This kind of innovation allows American fencers to develop their skill regardless of where they live. More fencers having access to good competitive opportunities is good for the growth and development of the sport.

Growth is a continued theme for the competitive fencing structure in the United States. There is a sense that there are always improvements to be had, always things that can be changed and updated to make the experience work better for fencers.

A broad experience

The multifaceted nature of fencing tournaments in the United States give American fencers a broad base of experience. There are a wide variety of tiers that give them the chance to solidify competition skills.

Access is a keyword here. The drive behind the competitive fencing structure in the United States is not a desire to collect international medals or to promote a certain ideology, rather it's a mission of personal development. This ties in with the university structure as well, as fencing in the United States encompasses a wide berth of skills and individuality with the goal of helping fencers to realize their potential holistically. That goes for fencers from all backgrounds and from all over the country.

A broad fencing experience, starting with local competitions and moving up through regional, divisional, and national competitions before jumping to the international venues allows fencers from America to be well prepared. As fencing competitions in the U.S. have become increasingly codified, that system has produced more potent and successful fencers. Up until university age, and sometimes even on into the university years, it's parents who give their children international level exposure. They travel on their own dime to European competitions (i.e., Cadet World Cups), travel the world for Junior World Cups, go to different international tournaments (for example, foil marathons in Paris for youth), and to camps, including international camps in Europe or China. While kids are young, they are exposed to this high level of competition, and it brings their game up dramatically. Obviously this kind of support requires a major financial commitment. When it's possible, it's a major boost.

Every fencing competition, whether it's one that leads to the Olympics or not, offers fencers a sense of pride and accomplishment. Healthy goal fulfillment is balanced with ambition through the competition system. It's not about the trophies. It's not about the podium. Those can be important pieces along the way, but they aren't the driving force. The competitive fencing tournament system in the United States isn't designed to crown winners, but to see who's best. It's designed to give fencers the opportunity to challenge themselves and grow through the sport. That system has the added benefit of boosting American fencers to international success.

The USFA has created a dynamic and supportive competitive structure. It's dynamic because it continues to evolve to make itself better, never content to adhere to the status quo for the regulation of this sport. Rule changes and tweaks to policies come every single year, all in a march towards excellence in fencing. The constant adaptation, creating new ways is important and USFA always improves.

It's supportive because the USFA offers a constant stream of accessible information for fencing families to access and for fencers to learn how to navigate the system. It's been exceedingly important that the competitive structure is something that novice fencers can enter into with ease, because it's in those early years of fencing competition that fencers become hooked into the system. Accessibility is key.

Chapter 11: Building on Success

The current wave of success that we see in American fencing has everything to do with building on the success of the past. It's never just me and my fencer, it's me learning from my coach who learned from their coach who learned from their coach before them. That word legacy, which sometimes sounds a bit puffed up when it's used in sports, can apply to the journey of American fencing. Maybe it's better if we call it generation learning in fencing, because each new crop of fencers is learning from the generation who came before us.

But how can American fencing keep the progress going? How do we take the momentum of the last two decades and forge a future of fencing that we want to see? That's a complex question with a complex answer.

This last year 2018 had arguably the best world championship performance by the American team, with two gold medals in women's foil and epee teams, and four podium finishes by Eli Derschwitz, Anna Stonem and Courtney Hurley, and the men's foil team, not to mention the top eight finishes of Curtis McDowland in epee, the men's foil team, and women's foil team claiming top world rankings. This is a fantastic result, one that we cannot ignore as a milestone in American fencing. As we've described in previous chapters, these milestones are part of a wider pattern of preparation and a long burn that's been simmering over a large arc of time. But as with every success in any field, the question is this a onetime fluke (even lasting last 15 years) or the beginning of great dominance?

A word that is often thrown around in American sports is "dynasty". In sports, a dynasty is a team that consistently wins titles over the course of many years, is filled with superstar talent, and has its own distinct personality. Think about the Edmonton Oilers with Wayne Gretzky, the LA Lakers with Magic Johnson and Kareem Abdul-Jabar, the New York Yankees with Babe Ruth and Lou Gehrig, or New England Patriots with Tom Brady and Bill Belichick. What these teams all have in common is their cohesiveness over a long period of time, with a synergy that builds momentum forward.

Fencing isn't perfectly analogous to pro sports, but the underlying sense is the same for all organized sports. Dynasties rise in American sports on the amateur level (think USA Gymnastics), on the college level (think Duke basketball or Notre Dame football), and on the high school level to a smaller scale around the country. The rise in American fencing over the last fifteen years has begun to take on the feel of a classic U.S. sports dynasty. It's not quite there, but the mouth to ear teaching necessary for high level fencing is building in that direction.

Our sport is unique among American sports for many reasons, but one thing that is the same is a deep desire to build a wide platform of success. A legacy.

Building by skill, not by the clock

Having one superstar fencer or even a handful of superstar fencers is not the way to create lasting success. By focusing on one athlete or even one coach, you're building a clock that will eventually wind its way down. In order to create a legacy for American fencing that can prosper in the long term, it must exist beyond the scope of a single individual or coach or club. Building a visionary fencing program for the United States is about the amalgamation of mastery in a broad swath - the output is the whole, not the part.

Top coaches in the most successful programs obviously want to create something that can sustain itself. The goals of each individual are going to necessarily take a backseat to the success of the program. What I've learned, and what I think many of you reading can appreciate, is that it is never about a particular coach or even a particular athlete. The number of medals, the level of fame, the money that might be made through endorsements, the building of an ego, none of this can matter for American fencing. What we want to drive us are consistent standards that stand the test of time. Partnership and team building, selflessness. As the water rises, so do all of the ships that are floating on it. When American fencing becomes better, those individual competitors and coaches will be better buoyed and able to reach their individual goals.

Doing away with medal counting

Yes, it's true that we've done a fair bit of medal counting here in this book. That's because it's necessary for us to measure success in some way and medals are an overt way to mark it. That's not just in fencing, but in any sport. You mark the progress with goals or homeruns or judge's scores. What we on the outside are doing to measure success must be very different from what the team on the inside is doing to achieve it!

Contrary to what many people think about elite athletes, the dominant and driving force is not getting to the top of the podium. It's got to be about skill mastery and love of the sport itself. The core of fencing has to transcend simply counting the number of medals around the neck of American fencers at the Olympic games, as proud as we may be to see our flag rise and hear our anthem play.

Points won and opponents defeated are not the main way that successful coaches use to judge either their effectiveness or the prowess of their fencers. It might sound a bit soft, but really what we're going for is human relationships and building up one another. Gold medals don't make a champion, it's heart and soul that make a champion. We see so many athletes who can make it to the top of the pile, but at what cost? Whether it's runaway doping, coaches who abuse athletes, or families who are torn apart by extreme training, the common thread is that when it's only the medals that are focus, we see negative consequences for real people. That's not how to build a sport and we're fortunate that it's not how we've seen American fencing grow.

Coach Mike Krzyzewski of Duke basketball said of his philosophy on winning, "Your definition of success should have more depth than the equivalent of winning a national championship." This is absolutely the way that American fencing has viewed its mission during its rise, and it's how things have to go forward. To that end, there are three things to keep in mind.

- Bring high quality people into American fencing
- Treat everyone involved, including opponents, with respect
- Mold an environment that encourages whole-person development (not just in fencing)

Notice that this takes the focus off of winning and places it squarely where it needs to be - on the people.

This does not mean that there are not giant, spectacular, larger than life goals. Clear, compelling goals are a focus point that unify team spirit in any sport. These are finish lines that people can see and reach. Our brains naturally attach themselves to targets, and the bigger the object it has to look at, the more emotionally motivating it can be. In the times of tough training or crippling losses, it's emotion that drives us through. When you've got clearly communicated goals, everyone knows immediately what they're supposed to be doing. That good emotional juice kicks in that keeps us going. Suddenly there's not a need to push an athlete when they're motivated by an objective from the inside out.

Goal setting has turned out to be a major boon to American fencing, a part of success that the United States has done remarkably well at in the last twenty years. By humanizing the pursuit of excellence, U.S. fencing coaches allow the people they coach to be the primary force. Setting goals that are focused on the individual's progress as a fencer rather than their outcome in the match is necessary.

Keep the essence, but keep progressing

American fencing can have the best philosophy and biggest talent, but if it refuses to change and grow then the success of the last few years will peter out. The core techniques that got it here should certainly be held on to, particularly the embracing of coaches steeped in knowledge, however the specifics must constantly be looked at for

To make a lasting legacy that keeps that success going takes a commitment to innovation. Stepping outside of the box while keeping one foot rooted in the precedents of this classical sport is how American fencing continues to move towards dominance. We can always do better. We can always find new ways. We can always grow. We can always adapt. That's the visionary future of American fencing.

As soon as we think that we've got all of the answers, it's time to change. Over the last hundred years of sport fencing, there has been a great deal of evolution from scoring with chalk to electric scoring, men only iterations to the full inclusion of women, refinement of right of way rule, and so much more. There is nothing static here, nothing stationary. As part of a sport that's growing and changing, American fencing has to grow as well. What we're looking for is not only to develop, but to mature at a pace that's at least a step ahead of rivals. Being open to new suggestions, outside recommendations, and even wisdom from the past is the way to do that.

Visionary culture

The spark of almost divine calling to success ties into the emotional component of success in sport. It's impossible to quantify the feeling of inspiration that has helped fencers to gain control over the course of international competition in recent years. American fencing has taken on an ethos that feels bigger than the individual while still valuing the individual athlete, and that's exactly the sense that must continue to build on these recent accomplishments.

There is no room in American fencing for athletes or coaches who do not adhere to the high ethics and training standards set forth in the last several decades. Though the environment in which these recent successes has incubated could hardly be called "comfortable" or "soft", at the same time it could hardly be called "hard" or "oppressive". Fencers knowingly step into this path, determining either that it's a good fit and something that they are passionate about pursuing, or that it isn't, and they can choose to walk away. Finding the balance of being both demanding and accepting is a constant struggle, but it's also the path to victory.

A major aspect of this is a pride in being a part of national fencing. The culture of United States fencing is one that's accepting of all races, national backgrounds, personal views, and lifestyle choices. Everyone is welcome in U.S. fencing if they are willing to put in the work and live out their passion for the sport. This can be seen in many ways, not the least of which is at Fencing Summer Nationals and other large competitions. There is always a sense of camaraderie when fencers from across the country come together. This is particularly important for young fencers coming up through the ranks to feel as it encourages them to stick with the sport. A culture that makes its athletes feel good is going to better attract good people.

Successful sporting cultures demand the best from their members. There is no tolerance for mediocrity, no allowance for slacking. That's across the board, in the club or during cross training, at home or in the classroom. This is about growing good people, not just good fencers.

Growing from within

Though this has been discussed in depth throughout this book, it's worth reiterating again. The careful selection and promotion of talent from within is how American fencing will continue to grow forward.

The wave of immigrant coaches from Soviet bloc countries boosted American fencing wonderfully from 1990's to today, however that influx is not going to happen in the same big numbers that it happened in before. American fencing is going to have to grow talent from within moving forward, and that's no small feat. Promotion from within, growing fencing coaches for future decades from the champions that we're seeing at the top of international podiums today, that's how we're going to make this success last.

This is something that American fencing can model on other sports for. When you look at dynamic, long lasting sports cultures at universities or professionally, often they are chock full of their own people. Think about how former professional football players go on to own NFL franchises. Michael Jordan (a native of North Carolina) bought the Carolina Hornets NBA team and has slowly been molding it into an increasingly winning franchise thanks to pouring his tremendous talent and understanding of the game into it. Internationally, look at World Cup player and coach Mario Zagallo of Brazil. He participated in four World Cup wins as either a coach or as a player. Or Joe Torre of the New York Yankees baseball team, who made nine All Star teams as a player and then managed the team to four World Series wins.

That's what fencing has got to do! Take the incredible talent that we've grown right here and leverage it forward for the future. We have seen this with Westbrook and Massialas as prominent examples of domestically raised coaches, and we will see more of this in the future.

No one knows the culture of American fencing like those who have risen through its successful ranks in the last two decades. It's those champions who hold the key to the future, in concert with the broad fencing organizations across the country who have built up young fencers in the last several decades.

Good enough can never be good enough

Nothing can ever be good enough. The quest for greatness has to continue ad infinitum.

This can sound harsh, but it's not nearly as harsh as it sounds if you think of fencing as a constant journey rather than as a destination. Nothing is ever good enough because life is ever changing, so our goals have to be ever changing.

"Are we winning?" changes to "How do we fence better tomorrow than we did today?" What happened this morning at the competition does not matter once it's over. All that matters is continuing to improve for the next competition. Satisfaction is impossible for a champion. The thirst for improvement is never slaked, regardless of the medals won or the accolades bestowed upon the athlete. Notice how this ties in beautifully to the previous philosophy we talked about - doing away with medal counting. If the mission is to win hardware, then the mission will fail. If the mission is to grow as a fencer, then the mission is possible.

There is no finish line.

Becoming and remaining a champion, visionary sports dynasty requires old fashioned hard work, discipline, and a deep rejection of smugness. At the highest levels of internationally competitive sports, there is no room for standing still. You are either moving forward or you're losing ground. There is constantly a competitor out to take your place on the podium, and that's an aspect of this journey that we welcome. It's part of what makes this rewarding! Those athletes who are ready to take on the challenge know that they must stay as close to the top of their game as possible at all times. A tough, consistent work ethic and smart practicing, buoyed by positive support is necessary for the success of American fencing from here on out.

Chapter 12: Challenges Ahead

The coming years will see a massive opportunity for American fencing, but how can we best take advantage of them? There are several challenges that stand in the way of preserving the momentum that's been created.

When we speak of challenges, we are looking towards the 2020 Olympics in Tokyo in just a bit over a year, but we're also looking far beyond that. This is a long game that we're playing with American fencing. There are no quick cuts, no short ways to make this happen. The fencers who are enrolling in our programs today are being built for the 2028 Olympics and the 2032 Olympics. We've spent a great deal of time looking back over the last twenty years in American fencing to chronicle it's rise, and as such it's worthwhile to look forward towards the next two decades of fencing in American to see how far we can go.

Lack of depth

There's a wide breadth to American fencing with schools across the country who have risen from varied backgrounds and styles. There is no one "style" of fencing in the United States, no specific school that you could point to identify the "American" fencing. That's a major strength, as we know that if an individual were to step away then the success could still remain through others.

What's missing in American fencing is the depth of knowledge. Where the fencing schools of Europe and even Russia are built upon many generations of learning, American fencing is still relatively new. We don't have a bank of champions and coaches to look back to. We as a nation of fencers have not yet proven that our fencing prowess will extend beyond the current group of tremendous fencers. Many of today's top fencers have been on top for years, and though fencing is blessed to have a long shelf life for its athletes, that's not going to be enough in the years to come.

Going forward, the United States has to learn ways to pass on the distinct styles and techniques that we've amassed over the last couple of decades in order to foster the kind of top fencing program that we are so eager to see. That means fencers coming back as coaches, schools continuing to innovate, and grooming a deep level of talent for the future. While we see this with some coaches that were made in America as athletes and coaches, some of whom we've written about here, there is still a dominating force of immigrants who are behind the push to greatness. It's not possible just yet for us to know with any kind of assurance that the coaching strength that exists currently among the coaches in the USA will pass on to the next generation of athletes as they grow to become coaches. It is just too soon to tell.

Another major challenge is that there is right now no such thing as 1st, 2nd, or 3rd national squad. What happens is that the gap between top fencers, say the top four to six, and the rest of the pack below them is massive. They aren't even in the same league. There is no depth to our current talent pool, and the gradient of fencing prowess in American fencing isn't a smooth curve but a sharp drop off. This indicates a lack of health in the system of training that we have in American fencing, one that will come back to haunt us competitively unless it is addressed and evened out.

Funding

This is a huge challenge for American fencing. It's impossible to overstate how much the funding structure of U.S. Olympic sports affects the way that training occurs here versus the way it occurs in other countries. This is something that we touched on earlier in reference to the past and the Soviet bloc countries, but it's still relevant today and will be in the future.

The United States Olympic Committee maintains a status as a 501(c)(3) non-profit corporation. It's not supported by the federal government or by state governments in any way, but rather entirely by individual American and corporate sponsors. It is truly a capitalist model for sport. Almost every other nation that competes in the Olympic Games provides at least some modicum of funding for its athletes.

In order for athletes to train and grow in fencing, they must figure out how to pay for it. It's important to note here that most internationally competitive fencers from the United States are adults who hold down professional jobs, often in highly skilled fields like medicine or law. The interplay of the American university fencing system is a key factor here, as education can afford fencers the opportunity to make more money in their careers and so have the flexibility to pay for training. At the same time, their attention is split between focusing on training and focusing on their career.

On a more mundane level, it's widely known that Olympic athletes often struggle with the financial demands of training. The burden of paying for travel, gear, coaching, entry fees, and simple daily life expenses is a large one. That stress isn't good for athletic performance, and there's little doubt that it affects America's ability to compete against countries whose athletes are able to focus more effectively on their training. Families of top athletes routinely go into debt in order to support their dream of competing in the Olympics. It's not a system that we can be proud of.

Winning can pay, though the numbers aren't as impressive as they might seem. U.S. Olympians in PyeongChang earned $37,500 for each gold medal, $22,500 for each silver and $15,000 for each bronze. For those competing in team events, the team members split the prize from the U.S. Olympic Committee. Considering that the plane ticket alone to travel internationally costs upwards of a thousand dollars, it's easy to see that the money evaporates quickly.

To be fair, the USFA does provide some support for the national team members. For example, the travel to international competitions is paid, as well as some salary from either USFA or USOC. Gear is often sponsored by fencing gear manufacturers, but this is mainly for a handful of top athletes, a half dozen at the very most, while the others aren't that supported and need to sustain themselves. Those who are on the top don't get large amounts, and certainly nothing on the order of what they would get as a salary in the private or even public sector.

Without sponsorships and some side gigs, like Imboden's and Chamley-Watson's modeling careers, it would be tough for them to survive. In Italy, for example, the salary of a professional fencer is large, twice as much as the average salary by some estimates. There's no doubt that they can make ends meet. As mentioned previously, they are generally employed through the police or army, so that after they retire from competitive career, they have a choice to continue their service with that government organization. We cannot discount the security of that arrangement, because it makes becoming a professional fencer a viable job option.

For American fencers, while they are in school that's ok, because there are sometimes school supports and sometimes parental. Once those fencers enter the adult life, priorities change of course. Funding now as well as long term financial security is extremely tough for our fencers. This lack of support structure is a potentially major reason that there is not a deeper pool of fencers that perform on a "professional" level in seniors.

Organizing and supporting fencers financially is a major issue. That's from the ground up. Some fencing schools in the United States offer scholarships for young fencers who could not afford to train without it, and that's a good start. Money should not be a barrier to athletic potential, and yet it very much is. The reality is that to run a fencing club requires capital, you must keep the lights on and the coaches fed. Many fencing clubs and coaches are working on reaching those fencers who would otherwise not be able to have access, but this is an area where we can grow. The better support we can give to our fencers to allow them to put their all into their performance, the more effectively they'll get to the top of that podium.

Over time, the resources that are poured into fencing pay dividends. Success draws people to anything, and as American fencing has seen more wins, we're also seeing more visibility and more young people coming in to start fencing! That higher level of visibility is the key to improved funding.

Another problem that we will face, though it might not materialize in the next decade, is the issue of coaching talent. The majority of it, at least as argued in the book, came from immigrants after the collapse of the USSR. While there are many great America-born coaches (Greg Massialas, Peter Westbrook, Dan Kelner, Sean McClain, Bucky Leach, etc.), there are definitely not enough to cover the whole country of fencers.

What will happen when the current wave of immigrant coaches retire? Who will continue the relay? Should we always rely on immigrants or there will be a natural raising the coaching talent and passing the legacy down? This is something that we've seen begin already, and it's an issue that will only become bigger. Coaches have a longer career than fencing athletes, but they can't go on forever. Somehow we will have to figure out how to fill the next generation.

Complacency

This is perhaps the biggest challenge ahead for American fencing. As we become more accustomed to being on top, it gets to be easier to assume that we belong there. Make no mistake - we don't belong on top if we don't keep fighting for it.

In the world of today, we sometimes see people looking for a magic wand like you see in the movies. A four-minute training montage where we see Rocky run up the steps of the Philadelphia Art Museum and chase some chickens, and then suddenly he's able to defeat Apollo Creed. Unfortunately, or perhaps fortunately, it doesn't work that way. There is no magic wand here, there's no John Candy to train your Jamaican bobsled team in a bathtub. It's all about smart work and hard work, work that keeps on going after the sun rises and sets again and again. The minute we stop working our hardest and our smartest, that's the minute that we'll see things fall apart. This is something that we've seen in other countries and with athletes in all disciplines. They start to win consistently and think that winning is just what they do.

If we have learned anything from our history, we must learn that those losses will come. The defeats are inevitable, and they are part of the beauty of sport. The difference in a champion program is that the bones are still there underneath. The feeder programs are still strong, the culture remains alive and well. With a firm foundation, every loss is recoverable and can in fact ignite the fire within us to train harder and move forward faster.

Chapter 13: Why American Fencing Matters

The value of American fencing goes well beyond the winning of medals or the accumulation of social media followers. What we as Americans bring to the sport is incredibly unique and important. What fencing as a sport brings to America is equally as unique and important. There is a beautiful interplay of relationships to be had here between athletes, young people, the international community, and communities all over the United States.

That same passion that we feel on the strip during a fencing bout has the potential to enliven and extend American's understanding of sport and to spark that same fire in the bellies of children (and adults) to give them happier and more well-rounded life experiences.

Real people

It's easy to sit back and view these athletes and their experiences as an "other", removed from our lives and existing in this almost fiction that's far away. After all, for most of us the Olympic Games or the International Fencing Championship are distant events that seem to have little effect on our own lives.

What we must learn to understand is that these are not far away, make believe events and people. Those fencing heroes that you read about and see beneath the rings at the Olympics?

You or your child could actually fence against them in a national level event much sooner than you imagine! Fencing is among the few sports where the heroes are totally approachable. They are here, among us, training in the same facility on the same ten club strips. They might fence in your pool in a next national tournament! Once upon a time they were just like you or your child, working to make headway in this sport of fencing that they have found a passion for. Top notch fencers are nothing more or less than real people who have honed in on a sport that is well matched to them and that they are disciplined enough to train hard in. Champions are real people.

Sports in general and fencing in particular matter! We have a responsibility as experienced fencers and as supportive parents to help create a path for the real-world people in America to get to fencing success that they are capable of.

This is the perfect situation to teach real kids about how to be persistent and patient, determined and courageous. By diving into competitive fencing, kids in America learn to work with others, to follow, to lead, to take responsibility for their actions or lack of actions, and so much more. Sports like fencing have this almost magical ability not only to develop better character in our youth, but to reveal the true nature of their character.

No matter what their ability level or challenges, every fencer in America has the opportunity to learn lifelong skills through this sport, and everyone has the right to do so. Youth fencing, and as importantly adult fencing, are places of development not only for athletic skills, but for life skills.

Real people making their real lives better through the real value of fencing in America.

Positive values and outcomes

This is where the rise of fencing in America takes an additional turn. Fencing does not teach character and values unless those lessons are intentionally taught by fencing coaches. Sports in general and fencing specifically offers us a golden opportunity to teach and maintain an egalitarian and holistic version of American values.

- Inclusion
- Independence
- Equality/egality
- Competition
- Work ethic
- Community
- Compassion
- Humility
- Integrity
- Perseverance
- Courage

American fencing is the best of these, when it's at its best. In fact, American culture is the best of these when it's at its best. Though there are myriad problems facing the United States, both from the inside and from the outside, what we can generally agree on is that the inner core of the American spirit is something to be prized. That's why immigrants flock here from all over the world, and it's why our American fencing team is so proud to walk beneath the stars and stripes at world competitions. We believe that the vision of America is one that is worthwhile, and that the values we espouse as part of this culture are worthwhile.

These are not values that our young people are going to learn on the Internet or through popular culture. Schools across America struggle under the crush of pressure and lack of funding, meaning they can't always teach these values. Parents are understandably concerned about how their children will learn to define themselves in a world that seems to value materialism and image. Wealth and fame cannot be the biggest goals that our children have, because if those are what youth are aiming for then they are being set up for a lifetime of disappointment and broken self-esteem. Yet how can one possibly compete with social media, movies, and peer pressures that tell young people to focus on their outward appearance and material possessions rather than their community?
A sword is hard to argue with.

Putting a fencing sword in the hand of a young woman or a young man shows them that their bodies have monumental autonomy. It shows them that they can use their minds to control their bodies and to reach goals that are far more exhilarating than any number of "likes" on a social media post. In a world of digital disconnection, fencing brings community and camaraderie. What makes fencing so special is that it combines the history and theatricality of sword fighting with the athleticism of the Olympics. The undercurrent of chivalry and integrity is still here in the 21st century! Tapping into that inner sensibility (it's always been there) leads to positive values and positive outcomes, both on the strip and beyond.

It's up to us to find other, more potent ways to pass them along to the next generation. Fencing is a powerful way to accomplish this necessary goal.

A future full of possibilities, rooted in integrity

Fencing, both for youth and for adults, offers a gateway to a future full of possibilities. We can see this in the gorgeous arc of success from the American fencing team over the last twenty years. Things that were once seen to be impossible, like multiple podium finishes at the Olympics for American fencers, or top rankings across weapons for American fencers in the World Fencing

Rankings, these things are now reality. That's come about through a long and hard road paved with long training days and monumental support.

American fencing is nothing short of an inspirational tale that galvanized the dreams of young fencers and their coaches to the point that they made those dreams into something they could touch.

One thing that marks American fencing as very different than other sports is that thus far, even as it has risen in the ranks of world competition, the slickness and focus on entertainment that has seeped into so many other popular American sports has not yet reached fencing. The tropes that plague other youth sports such as parental overpressure, stress for college admission or funding, a focus on winning at all costs, extreme social pressure, ingrained bullying, etc., aren't a part of American fencing. Even at the national level, fencing remains rooted in integrity and community. Our highest-ranking athletes have a bend towards humility and accessibility, in part because of the niche nature of the sport, but also because of the honorable nature of fencing. A loss is nothing to be ashamed of, an opponent is not an enemy, and the cap on our achievement only exists insofar as we limit ourselves.

There is a great potential for fencing to transform the lives of people who would not otherwise have access to it as the sport spreads further and further throughout America.

Fencing as an art

Perhaps what makes fencing the most unique is that it is not just a sport, it's an art form. While yes, all sports have their own beauty about them, there is something patently different about fencing. Whereas other sports started off for recreation, there has always been a mystique about sword fighting that is so much more than a game. It is this capacity that elevates fencing to an art form, rather than simply being another ball trying to go into a goal.

We are learning as fencers to both harness and extol the inherent yearning for domination within our spirits. It's a drive that we can capture, one that is too often misguided towards control and using other people. Instead what we find in fencing is the ability to go for that point, to indulge our deep need to compete and so satisfy our visceral nature, while at the same time engaging our big human minds to get there without sacrificing our integrity.

Fencing both reveals and develops character, it tells us who we are and shows us how to grow. This happens as a natural part of competition with any sport but fencing offers its athletes layers of complexity and tradition that extend further down than other sports. It's simultaneously innovative and traditional, physical and mental. We are partaking in the best of ourselves.

Fencing has the potential to change lives. Just ask Peter Westbrook or Ibtihaj Muhammad. But you don't have to go all the way to the Olympic level. When someone becomes a fencer, even for a short period of time, it tends to have a profound and lasting impact on their lives. The uniqueness of our sport is beautiful! There really is nothing like it anywhere else. Ask someone who fenced for just a season, or even just a few lessons, and they will remember it vividly. Something about the combination of the sword and the lines of movement, the fearlessness of combat and the camaraderie of the match hangs in the air long after we leave the club. It's instinctual, the drive for children to pick up sticks and pretend to swordfight.

The courage that a fencer must muster to step on that strip with a sword, whether it's for the first time or the thousandth time, is remarkable. Though we know that we are safe from harm, the rush of energy that fuels combat is beyond that of another sport. Even martial arts, with the control and precision, cannot unleash the same primal instincts as fencing and remain safe. When we talk about the American spirit of conquest and channeling that for a positive outcome, fencing is a perfect match of raw energy and refined ideology. It's balance and then some. It's art.

The future of fencing in America is bright and full of possibilities. The question is not one of potential, but what we decide to do with that potential. It's all up to us, and there's nothing more exciting than that.

Appendix A - USA International Competition Results

Olympic Fencing Country Rankings

\multicolumn{6}{c}{Olympic Women's Fencing Country Rankings 1924-2016}
Rank	Country	Gold	Silver	Bronze	Total
1	Italy	11	8	8	27
2	Hungary	8	6	7	21
3	Russia	6	3	2	11
4	Soviet Union	5	3	2	10
5	France	4	3	5	12
6	West Germany	3	2	1	6
7	Germany	2	5	3	10
8	Romania	2	4	4	10

| 9 | China | 2 | 4 | 3 | 9 |
| 10 | United States | 2 | 2 | 5 | 9 |

Olympic Men's Fencing Country Rankings 1896-2016					
Rank	Country	Gold	Silver	Bronze	Total
1	France	37	37	29	103
2	Italy	37	34	25	96
3	Hungary	29	17	20	66
4	Soviet Union	13	12	14	39
5	Cuba	6	5	6	17
6	Russia	6	2	5	13
7	Poland	4	8	7	19
8	West Germany	4	6	0	10
9	Belgium	3	3	4	10
10	Germany	3	2	6	11

11	Sweden	2	3	2	7
12	China	2	3	0	5
13	Romania	2	1	3	6
14	Greece	2	1	1	4
15	South Korea	2	0	3	5
16	United States	1	7	11	19

Olympic Fencing Medal Detail United States

2004 Athens			
Women's Individual Sabre	Gold	Mariel Zagunis	Silver - China
Women's Individual Sabre	Bronze	Sada Jacobson	
2008 Beijing			
Women's	Gold	Mariel Zagunis	

Individual Sabre			
Women's Individual Sabre	Silver	Sada Jacobson	
Women's Individual Sabre	Bronze	Rebecca Ward	
Women's Team Sabre	Bronze	Mariel Zagunis, Sada Jacobson, Rebecca Ward	Gold - Ukraine Silver - China
Women's Team Foil	Silver	Erinn Smart, Hanna Thompson, Emily Cross	Gold - Russia Bronze - Italy
Men's Team Sabre	Silver	Tim Morehouse, Jason Rogers, Keeth Smart, James Williams	Gold - South Korea

				Bronze - Italy
\multicolumn{5}{c}{2012 London}				
Women's Team Epee	Bronze	Courtney Hurley, Kelley Hurley, Maya Lawrence, Susie Scanlan	Gold - China Silver - South Korea	
\multicolumn{5}{c}{2016 Rio}				
Women's Team Sabre	Bronze	Ibtihaj Muhammad, Dagmara Wozniak, Mariel Zagunis, Monica Aksamit	Gold - Russia Silver - Ukraine	
Men's Individual Foil	Silver	Alexander Massialas	Gold - Italy Bronze - Russia	
Men's Team	Bronze	Miles Chamley-	Gold -	

| Foil | | Watson, Race Imboden, Alexander Massialas, Gerek Meinhardt | Russia

Silver - France |
|---|---|---|---|
| Men's Individual Sabre | Silver | Daryl Homer | Gold - Hungary

Bronze - South Korea |

Fencing World Championships Country Rankings

Fencing World Championships Country Rankings 1937-2018					
Rank	Country	Gold	Silver	Bronze	Total
1	Italy	118	102	124	344
2	Hungary	90	84	94	268
3	Soviet Union	90	57	50	197
4	France	89	97	95	281
5	Russia	53	26	37	116
6	West Germany	25	26	14	65
7	Germany	22	29	39	90
8	Poland	17	29	39	85
9	Romania	13	25	28	66
10	Ukraine	11	11	15	37
11	United States	9	12	10	31

12	China	7	18	17	42
13	Sweden	7	13	17	37
14	South Korea	6	11	19	36
15	Cuba	6	5	9	20

United States Junior World Fencing Championship Medals

	Junior World Fencing Championship
2000	Women's Individual Foil - Iris Zimmerman
2001	Women's Team Sabre
2001	Men's Team Sabre
2001	Women's Individual Sabre - Mariel Zagunis
2003	Women's Individual Sabre - Sada Jacobson
2004	Women's Individual Sabre - Sada Jacobson
2004	Women's Team Sabre

2005	Women's Individual Sabre - Mariel Zagunis
2005	Women's Team Sabre
2005	Men's Team Sabre
2005	Women's Individual Foil - Emily Cross
2006	Women's Individual Sabre - Mariel Zagunis
2006	Women's Team Sabre
2006	Men's Team Sabre
2006	Women's Individual Foil - Emily Cross
2008	Men's Team Foil
2009	Women's Individual Epee - Kelley Hurley
2009	Women's Team Epee
2010	Men's Team Foil
2011	Men's Team Foil
2011	Women's Individual Foil Nzingha Prescod
2012	Men's Team Foil
2013	Men's Individual Foil Alexander Massialas

2013	Women's Team Sabre
2014	Women's Individual Foil - Lee Kiefer
2015	Women's Individual Foil - Sara Taffel
2015	Women's Team Foil
2015	Men's Individual Sabre - Eli Dershwitz
2016	Women's Individual Foil - Sabrina Massialas
2017	Men's Team Foil
2018	Women's Team Foil
2018	Men's Individual Foil - Nick Itkin
2019	Women's Individual Foil – Lauren Scruggs

Appendix B - Unified Sports Classification System

- Merited Master of Sport of the USSR, (an international champion who has made significant contributions to the sport)
- Master of Sport of the USSR, International Class (an international champion)
- Master of Sport of the USSR (national champion)
- Candidate for Master of Sport of the USSR (an athlete with national rank)
- First-Class Sportsman (a regional champion)
- Second-Class Sportsman (a state champion)
- Third-Class Sportsman (a city champion)
- First-Class Junior Sportsman (a regional youth champion)
- Second-Class Junior Sportsman (a state youth champion)
- Third-Class Junior Sportsman (a city youth champion)

Appendix C - References

BBC. (2011). "Blood and Sweat at a Russian Sports School". *BBC*. 14 November 2011. Retrieved from http://www.bbc.co.uk/worldclass/15718101

Blau, I. (2013). "Ideology of Soviet Sport". Boston University: Guided History. Retrieved from http://blogs.bu.edu/guidedhistory/russia-and-its-empires/ian-blau/

Blom, L. (2013) "Maximizing the Benefits of Youth Sport". *Journal of Physical Education, Recreation & Dance* 84:7, 8-13.

Caroccioli, T. & Caroccioli, J. (2008). *Boycott: Stolen Dreams of the 1980 Moscow Olympic Games*. Highland Park, IL: New Chapter Press.

Douglas-Gabriel, D. (2017). "Families are paying more out of pocket for college as tuition increases surpass grant aid". *The Washington Post*. 25 October 2017.

Elkins, K. (2018). "Here's how much US Olympic medalists get paid". *CNBC*. 16 February 2018. Retrieved from https://www.cnbc.com/2018/02/16/how-much-olympic-athletes-get-paid.html

Greene, B. (2012). "What changed the Olympics forever". *CNN.* 23 July 2012. Retrieved from http://www.cnn.com/2012/07/22/opinion/greene-olympics-amateurs/index.html

Harris, C. (2016). "Blades of Glory: Meet Our Black Olympian Fencers". *Essence.* 12 August 2016.

Hickey, J. (2014)."Athletes recall 1980 Olympic boycott". *San José Mercury News.* 21 January 2014.

Kirby, J. (2016). "New York's Olympic Sport Is Fencing". *The Intelligencer: New York Magazine.* Retrieved from http://nymag.com/intelligencer/2016/08/new-yorks-olympic-sport-is-fencing.html

NFCR. (2016). "The Distribution of Men's and Women's Rating Classifications by Weapon at Year End 31 July 2012 – 31 July 2015". *National Fencing Club Rankings.* Retrieved from http://nationalfencingclubrankings.com/the-distribution-of-mens-and-womens-rating-classifications-by-weapon-at-year-end-31-july-2012-31-july-2015/

Taylor, A. (2012). "Here's How Much Olympic Athletes Really Get Paid". *Business Insider*. 19 July 2012.

Taylor, P. (2004). *Jews and the Olympic Games: The Clash Between Sport and Politics: With a Complete Review of Jewish Olympic Medalists*. Sussex Academic Press.

USOC. (1972). *1972 United States Olympic Book*. United States Olympic Committee. New York, New York

Made in the USA
Monee, IL
10 December 2021